# ART & SOUL

## WEST VIRGINIANS *in the* ARTS

**An APPALACHIAN EDUCATION INITIATIVE Book**

**Design**
Bryan Boyd Creative Group, Inc.
Charleston, West Virginia

**Editors**
Brooke A. Brown & Jennifer Francis Alkire

**Design Editor**
C. Todd Thomas

**Project Coordinator and Artist Liaison**
Brooke A. Brown

**Thanks**
The Andy Griffith Show Rerun Watchers Club Archive, Stacey Angel, Robert Bridges, Charleston Magazine, Mark Crabtree, John Cuthbert, Richard Currey, Fairmont State University, Goldenseal Magazine, Grand Ole Opry, Huntington Quarterly, Jackson Kelly/Attorneys at Law, Kate Long, Marshall University, McJunkin Corporation, National Endowment for the Arts, University of North Carolina – Chapel Hill Outdoor Drama Department, Scott Rotruck, West Virginia Commission on the Arts, West Virginia Department of Education and the Arts, West Virginia Division of Culture & History, West Virginia Film Office, West Virginia Public School System, West Virginia University and the 50 featured artists and/or their assistants, representatives and management.

Published in 2005 by the Appalachian Education Initiative. All rights reserved.

Printed and bound by Morgantown Printing & Binding, USA.

ISBN 0-9767021-0-X

**Appalachian Education Initiative**
111 High Street
Morgantown, West Virginia 26505
www.appalachianeducationinitiative.org

*The young do not know enough to be prudent, and therefore they attempt the impossible – and achieve it, generation after generation.*

–Pearl Buck

Where does inspiration come from?  Is it all around us, just waiting to be tapped by our imaginations, or is it in the hands of someone else – a mentor or teacher whose gift we all hope to receive?  The answers are as diverse and varied as the incredible talents highlighted in this book.

*Art & Soul: West Virginians in the Arts* celebrates the successes of performing, literary and visual artists who attended a West Virginia public school for at least some portion of their K-12 education. Both an educational and inspirational tool, *Art & Soul* is part of a campaign led by the Appalachian Education Initiative to raise awareness for the importance of arts education in our public schools and communities.

By showcasing individuals who received their education and early arts-related exposure in West Virginia and who ultimately achieved great success as professional artists, *Art & Soul* promises to raise awareness of the vital role the arts play in every child's personal development. Also, parents will be encouraged to take the necessary steps to ensure that their children are receiving enriching arts education opportunities in the public schools. Education administrators will be encouraged to make arts education a priority in academic curriculum. Concerned citizens will be encouraged to participate in charitable giving to support arts education programming. And young artists will be inspired by the demonstrated success of others to set high goals and to work hard to achieve them.

This is one of three planned volumes of *Art & Soul* to be published over the next seven years. Each volume will highlight new and different artists with the hope of including as many West Virginia artists as possible. The theme of this volume is "Notable and Noteworthy," featuring artists who have become recognized far beyond West Virginia's borders.

The 50 artists selected for this edition were nominated by various statewide arts organizations, the West Virginia Film Office and even some of the artists, themselves. The list was reviewed in collaboration with the West Virginia Commission on the Arts. Great care was taken to achieve a representative sample both across the various art forms and geographically and is in no way intended to be an exhaustive representation of the artistic talent that West Virginia has procured.

To invite nominations for the next volume of *Art & Soul,* or to order additional copies of the book, please visit our website at www.appalachianeducationinitiative.org and click on *Art & Soul.*

But for now, explore the pages that follow and get to know a little bit more about some of West Virginia's finest talents. You'll find that inspiration is abundant in West Virginia, from Wheeling to Welch, Charleston to Charles Town, and that it's a resource well worth maintaining.

Sincerely,

*Jennifer Francis Alkire*

Jennifer Francis Alkire, President & CEO
Appalachian Education Initiative

A Foreword by Richard Currey

*While my West Virginia family had its share of big storytellers, it was my grandfather who introduced me to books and writers, from Daniel Defoe to Charles Dickens, Hemingway and Steinbeck. I became a voracious reader and a budding, if very private, young writer. The entire business around books and writing was a shared secret between my grandfather and me. Why a secret? Because both of us, I later realized, were operating under the presumption that being a West Virginian and a creative artist were incompatible. The two just didn't fit together. Still, my grandfather seemed to have something in mind that flew in the face of that conventional wisdom.*

One day in the spring of 1959, my grandfather took me to something called an "arts fair" held at the high school in my home town of Parkersburg. I had no idea what an arts fair might entail. But on that bright afternoon I saw (and heard) the creative efforts of other young people, West Virginians all. Here were drawings and paintings and sculptures and photographs, elegant poems carefully written in a best cursive and placed on display, a student-written-and-performed play in progress in a classroom temporarily redone as a theatre, and, in the main auditorium, another student conducted the high school orchestra in a piece that she had composed. I was more than surprised or impressed – I was disoriented. Clearly the creative arts and an Appalachian bloodline were not mutually exclusive. Looking back, thinking of the moments in a life that may have been actually pivotal in some way, I believe that afternoon told me a great deal about the possibility and potential for realizing a creative gift, no matter where I might have been born.

It is very significant to note that the high school arts fair was enabled by a school and its teachers. It was a vivid expression of the faith those teachers carried in both the importance of their students' efforts as well as the various potentials those efforts implied. If I can credit a West Virginia school event for lighting a quiet fire somewhere inside me, then

> *"If I can credit a West Virginia school event for lighting a quiet fire somewhere inside me, then that credit necessarily falls to a group of teachers who stood behind their students and provided a forum, an opportunity, a chance."*

that credit necessarily falls to a group of teachers who stood behind their students and provided a forum, an opportunity, a chance. It suggested to me, another West Virginia kid but only a random visitor that day, that similar opportunities might be available in my life as well.

Not that ten or two or even one of those students whose work was represented that day went on to a career in the arts. Producing professional artists is, in a certain sense, simply a potential added benefit of healthy arts education programs. Arts in the schools make a much broader contribution to human development and educational success, forging the sort of imaginative and problem-solving skills that any family, employer or society values above almost all other attributes. And this assertion is not simply my surmise or a well-intentioned hunch; it is research-proven across studies dating back 35 years in the open scientific literature. This research has amply demonstrated that arts education and opportunities to participate in the arts

enhance a range of abilities, and in measurable ways, as completely as do courses in science, mathematics and social studies. Beyond that, some of the capacities we collectively mourn a decline in – integrity, tolerance, empathy – are demonstrably enhanced through arts education. So, why, then, does arts education get short shrift in policy and budgetary planning, particularly in areas like West Virginia and the mountain south where education should be a highest priority?

The answers, of course, cross a range of dueling political, bureaucratic, and financial agendas. The arts education problem is compounded in West Virginia and the cultural island of Appalachia, where the notion that creative artists neither rise nor prevail still seems to be common currency. If we want to engender widespread support for arts education, we must first understand that our home State has already produced some of the most important and well-known creative artists of the last half-century. A formidable start to that effort is the

book that you hold in your hands. *Art & Soul: West Virginians in the Arts* profiles 50 of the State's most important and best-known artists, and I guarantee that you will be surprised, pleased and proud to see the nature and extent of West Virginia's artistic contributions, spanning theatre, film and television, literature, dance, every kind of music from country to classical and every manner of visual art.

Any superlative one might think of easily applies to the 50 individuals you will meet in these pages. World-famous, legendary, profoundly accomplished, prolific, influential – they're all here. Film and TV stars or country music greats? Best-selling authors, prize-winning poets, screenwriters and movie directors? Opera stars, geniuses of sculpture, painting and dance? Read on. They hail from every town, city and crossroads in the State of West Virginia, and their collective contributions make for a stunning national treasure. *Art & Soul* tells their individual stories, just as it reminds us that, when it comes to arts and arts education, West Virginia need only keep up the good work.

*Richard Currey*

# Richard Currey

West Virginia native RICHARD CURREY is the award-winning author of the novels *Lost Highway* and *Fatal Light*, and the West Virginia-based short story collection *The Wars of Heaven*.  A writer who often refers to West Virginia and Appalachia as his "mythic ground," Currey is a recipient of two National Endowment for the Arts Fellowships, the D. H. Lawrence Fellowship, O. Henry and Pushcart Prizes for short story excellence, a Special Citation of the Hemingway Foundation and many other honors.  His books have been published in 11 foreign languages and more than 20 different editions around the world.

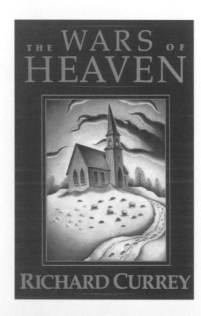

The Parkersburg-born writer launched his career in the early 1970s, and has since seen his work in many of the nation's leading magazines and newspapers.  His work has been performed on stage at Symphony Space in New York, aired on National Public Radio and included in the Gabriel Award-winning West Virginia Public Radio series *In Their Own Country*.

Currey's novel *Lost Highway* has been re-issued in a fully re-designed edition by WVU Press, and released as an audiobook – complete with original music – by Martinsburg's Mountain Whispers.

In 1998 Currey was awarded the State of West Virginia's Daugherty Award in the Humanities for "life-long contributions to West Virginia humanities and culture."

TOP, LEFT ]
*The Wars of Heaven* (1990).

LEFT ] *Crossing Over* (1993).

# Art & Soul | Volume One

# Maggie Anderson

MAGGIE ANDERSON was born in New York City in 1948 to parents with roots in Appalachia. Her mother grew up on a farm in southwestern Pennsylvania and her father was the son of railroad workers from Preston County, West Virginia. Both of her parents were teachers.

When Maggie was nine years old, her mother died of leukemia, and in 1959 she and her father moved back to West Virginia. She attended sixth grade and junior high school in Buckhannon; in 1964 they moved to the eastern panhandle, where Maggie graduated from Keyser High School in 1966.

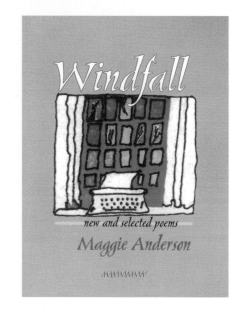

Maggie earned her B.A. and M.A. degrees in English at West Virginia University. In 1971, while still living in Morgantown, she founded the poetry journal, *Trellis*, with Winston Fuller and current West Virginia Poet Laureate, Irene McKinney.

Marshall County was the site of Maggie's first job as poet-in-the-schools in 1979. Over the next ten years, she worked in schools, senior centers, correctional facilities and libraries in West Virginia, Ohio and Pennsylvania. After several visiting writer positions at universities, including the University of Pittsburgh and the University of Oregon, Maggie began teaching creative writing at Kent State University in 1989 and is currently on the faculty of the Northeast Ohio Universities Master of Fine Arts program.

Maggie Anderson's chapbook, *The Great Horned Owl*, was published in 1979. Her first full-length collection of poems, *Years That Answer*, appeared in 1980 and was followed by three others, including *Windfall: New and Selected Poems* in 2000. Recent essays have been published in *Liberating Memory: Work and Our Working-Class Consciousness* (1995) and in *Bloodroot: Reflections on Place by Appalachian Women Writers* (1998).

Maggie is the editor of *Hill Daughter: New and Selected Poems* by former West Virginia Poet Laureate, Louise NcNeill, and co-editor of *Learning by Heart: Contemporary American Poetry about School* and *A Gathering of Poets*, an anthology of poems commemorating the 20th anniversary of the shootings of students in an anti-war protest at Kent State University in 1970.

# HOMETOWN
## West Virginia

### KEYSER

## FROM THE SOUL

Since 1992, Maggie has directed the Wick Poetry Center and edited the Wick Poetry Series published by the Kent State University Press. She has twice won Distinguished Teaching awards and was recognized as a Distinguished Scholar in 2004. Also in 2004, the Wick Poetry Program celebrated its 20th anniversary with the creation of a new Center with a $2 million endowment in the College of Arts & Sciences.

In September 2004, Emory & Henry College honored Maggie Anderson at their twenty-third annual Literary Festival. Additional honors and awards over the last twenty years include two fellowships in poetry from the National Endowment for the Arts and grants from the Ohio Arts Council and the MacDowell Colony. Maggie has had poems in nearly 40 anthologies and textbooks, as well as many poetry journals.

OPPOSITE, LEFT ] *Windfall: New and Selected Poems* (2000).

TOP, LEFT ] Maggie working with deaf and hearing impaired students at McMechen Elementary School in McMechen, West Virginia (1978).

ABOVE ] A sketch from Maggie's journal.

What I recall most clearly from my seven years of public school in West Virginia is the view from the windows of each of my classrooms. How I managed to be a good student while also a persistent daydreamer puzzles me. Yet somehow I did keep my grades up (and, in fact, graduated among the top ten students in my class) while gazing out the windows for extended periods of time from the sixth grade through high school. The hills outside the window held my attention, as they changed color and shape with the seasons, the weather, and the light.

The teachers I had in New York before moving to West Virginia had reprimanded me severely for what they saw as my inattention. My teachers in West Virginia did not seem to mind as much. As long as I stayed moderately alert to the subject at hand, they were tolerant, or at least they did not nag me. Most of them made spaces during class time for reflection, for quiet, and for children to be left alone.

Daydreaming is essential to the creative process. Only through the necessary hours of staring off into space doing nothing can the imagination be called into being. Several of my teachers encouraged me to write about what I saw outside the window. This not only gave permission to my "inattention," but it also brought the outside world into the classroom and made it, through the act of writing, a part of our work. I do not know how possible this is in *any* classroom in this country today, but I remember and honor my West Virginia teachers for the freedom they allowed me to dream and to write off the subject, in the margins of the lesson plan.

*Maggie Anderson*

# Stephen Coonts

STEPHEN COONTS is the author of 13 New York Times bestsellers, the first of which was the classic flying tale, *Flight of the Intruder.*

Born in 1946, Stephen Paul Coonts grew up in Buckhannon, West Virginia, a coal-mining town of 6,000 population on the western slope of the Appalachian mountains. He majored in political science at West Virginia University, graduating in 1968 with an A.B. degree. Upon graduation he was commissioned an Ensign in the U.S. Navy and began flight training in Pensacola, Florida.

He received his Navy wings in August, 1969. After completion of fleet replacement training in the A-6 Intruder aircraft, Mr. Coonts reported to Attack Squadron 196 at NAS Whidbey Island, Washington. He made two combat cruises aboard USS Enterprise during the final years of the Vietnam War as a member of this squadron. After the war he served as a flight instructor on A-6 aircraft for two years, then did a tour as an assistant catapult and arresting gear officer aboard USS Nimitz. He left active duty in 1977 and moved to Colorado. After short stints as a taxi driver and police officer, he entered the University of Colorado School of Law in the fall of 1977.

Mr. Coonts received his law degree in December, 1979, and moved to West Virginia to practice. He returned to Colorado in 1981 as a staff attorney specializing in oil and gas law for a large independent oil company.

# HOMETOWN
## West Virginia

### BUCKHANNON

His first novel, *Flight Of The Intruder*, published in September, 1986, by the Naval Institute Press, spent 28 weeks on the New York Times bestseller list in hardcover. A motion picture based on this novel, with the same title, was released nationwide in January, 1991.

The success of his first novel allowed Mr. Coonts to devote himself full time to writing; he has been at it ever since. He and his wife, Deborah, enjoy flying and try to do as much of it as possible.

Mr. Coonts' books have been widely translated and republished in the British Commonwealth, France, Germany, The Netherlands, Finland, Sweden, Denmark, Italy, Spain, Mexico, Brazil, Turkey, Poland, Bulgaria, Hungary, Russia, China, Japan, Czechoslovakia, Serbia and Israel.

Mr. Coonts was a trustee of West Virginia Wesleyan College from 1990-1998. He was inducted into the West Virginia University Academy of Distinguished Alumni in 1992. The U.S. Naval Institute honored him with its Author of the Year Award for

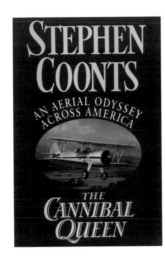

the year 1986 for his novel, *Flight Of The Intruder*. Mr. Coonts and his wife, Deborah, reside in Las Vegas, Nevada.

OPPOSITE, TOP ] Steve and the Cannibal Queen at the old Lewis Field (now closed) in Buckhannon, West Virginia.

OPPOSITE, RIGHT ] *Flight of the Intruder* (1986)

ABOVE ] *The Cannibal Queen (1992)*

## FROM THE SOUL

After living all over America and sending four children to schools in four states, I have come to value an attribute from my Upshur County, West Virginia, public school education that didn't seem unusual at the time. The schools weren't surburbanized or homogenized. The junior high and high school were the only ones in the county, so all the kids went there; we had youngsters who had graduated from one-room grade schools out in the county and the city grade schools. We had the sons and daughters of miners, mine owners, truck drivers, car dealers, doctors, lawyers, plumbers, police, secretaries, the addicted, the unemployed and the unemployable. In short, I went to school with everybody, rich and poor, black and white. And afterwards they went everywhere. They grew up and marched on to every profession and trade, made all the mistakes... lived their lives well or screwed them up, got them straightened out or didn't. It was a great education. It equipped me for seven years of college, for the military, for a profession, gave me a foundation that I could build on to become a writer, gave me a foundation for life.

That's what education is supposed to do, isn't it?

# William F. DeVault

**101**
*Great Love Poems*

from the works of The Romantic Poet of the Internet,
**William F. DeVault**

The new renaissance is alive and well, and as with any exponential explosion of human expression and creativity, there are figures who follow the path, and those who blaze it.

WILLIAM F. DEVAULT has been called "the future of the digital renaissance" by overseas literary magazines, but he is more one of the fathers, the trailblazers. While now you can hardly swing a mousepad without hitting a writers' website or poetry corner on the world-wide web, it was he who was christened the *Romantic Poet of the Internet* by Yahoo in the mid-nineties. He who was a co-founder for the legendary *Poets Place* on America Online.

Born in Greenville, South Carolina, into a military family, he found himself drifting from state to state, never establishing roots outside of his family, until his father's retirement from the Air Force and their subsequent return to his hometown, Morgantown, West Virginia.

The same father who read his sons and daughter the classics at naptime and fostered their interest in the literary arts brought them back to a town that, although located in a state often the butt of jokes decrying its lack of sophistication, was both scholarly and international, thanks to the presence of West Virginia University.

It was there that he turned a knack for wordsmithing into a gift for "cathartic expression" and developed a knack for extemporaneous and single-draft verse that propelled him into the spotlight years later.

Having written his first verse at age eight, he played with his gift as merely a sideline, something to be amused by,

like juggling or a green thumb. But, when he was a student at Morgantown High School, he wrote his first romantic verse to a classmate he was smitten by and discovered how potent a weapon, how effective a tool for communicating out of a shy adolescent. His catalog of thousands of works, including such cult favorites as *The Panther Cycles, the patchwork*

# HOMETOWN
### West Virginia

### MORGANTOWN

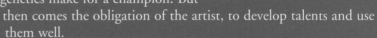

## FROM THE SOUL

*Kiss not the sky for I am home, before you, and I would be jealous of each cloud, and I am proud, but not so much that I cannot admit I want you.*

*skirt of my love* and *Triumph* have mesmerized audiences around the world, garnering him a following in many lands.

Although he spent many of the past several years on the West Coast, he himself predicted in his "prophecy" work, *Horizon,* that "the winds of an old rage" would yet "blow me East." Back to West Virginia.

And now he is back in the Mountain State, preparing his next books, touring, lecturing and readying himself for the stage upon which his talent has thrust him.

OPPOSITE, LEFT ] *101 Great Love Poems* (2002)

ABOVE ] *The Morgantown Suite* (2005)

I learned my craft as a catharsis, as a coping mechanism for dealing with the hard hands dealt by fate. That I have the words to express myself, to impress others, is no more to my credit than an athlete's natural abilities are to his or her's. Good coaching and good genetics make for a champion. But then comes the obligation of the artist, to develop talents and use them well.

Had I been raised in ivory tower isolation, nurtured but unchallenged, I may have grown as a bonsai man, pruned to the skills of a gardener who knew only the cookie-cutter regimentation they had been taught. But, as I was allowed to grow inside of a culture and a community (Morgantown) that was real and living, I was able to grow as a tree in a forest, into a natural thing, an honest facet in the expression of the ongoing evolution of life under the watchful eye of a divine Creator.

I must give credit to my 9th grade Creative Writing teacher, Mrs. Tomasky, who challenged and opened my mind and eyes to colours of spectrums I was not already exposed to and aware of. I hope she forgives my arrogance and occasional bouts of impudence. I thank her for her time and skills while I was at Morgantown Junior High School. Also, many thanks to Miss McConnell, Mrs. Stevens and Mrs. Yagle for their contributions at Morgantown High. The best artist is wasted without the tools to work with. I hope you are at least sometimes pleased with what I have done with the *wordblades* and *thoughthammers* you gave me.

# Henry Louis Gates, Jr.

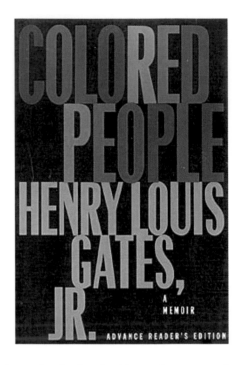

HENRY LOUIS GATES, JR. was raised in the small, Mineral County town of Piedmont, West Virginia. His father, Henry Louis Sr., worked at the local paper mill during the day and at a telephone company as a janitor at night. Gates' mother, Pauline Coleman Gates, cleaned houses and worked hard to give her sons the self-confidence to live in an integrated world.

Gates attended the local Piedmont schools – schools that had been desegregated only a year before he began the first day – and excelled academically, graduating at the top of his high school class in 1968. From there he attended Potomac State College, a branch of West Virginia University, with plans to go to medical school. Those plans changed when he took courses in American and English literature from Professor Duke Anthony Whitmore. His influence encouraged Gates to apply to the Ivy League schools.

He earned his M.A. and Ph.D. in English Literature from Clare College at the University of Cambridge. He received a B.A. *summa cum laude* from Yale University in 1973 in History. Before joining the faculty of Harvard in 1991, he taught at Yale, Cornell and Duke Universities. Gates is currently the W. E. B. Du Bois Professor of the Humanities, Harvard University, Chair of the Department of African and African American Studies and Director of the W. E. B. Du Bois Institute for African and African American Research.

Professor Gates is co-editor with K. Anthony Appiah of the encyclopedia *Encarta Africana* published on CD-ROM by Microsoft (1999), and in book form by Basic Civitas Books under the title *Africana: The Encyclopedia of the African and African American Experience* (1999). He is the author of *Wonders of the African*

## HOMETOWN
### West Virginia

PIEDMONT

*World* (1999), the book companion to the six-hour BBC/PBS television series of the same name. He is also the author of *America Behind the Color Line: Dialogues with African Americans* (2004), written to accompany the PBS documentary with the same title.

Professor Gates is the author of several works of literary criticism, including *Figures in Black: Words, Signs and the Racial Self* (Oxford University Press, 1987); *The Signifying Monkey: A Theory of Afro-American Literary Criticism* (Oxford, 1988), 1989 winner of the American Book Award; and *Loose Canons: Notes on the Culture Wars* (Oxford, 1992). He has also authored *Colored People: A Memoir* (Knopf, 1994), which traces his childhood experiences in a small West Virginia town in the 1950s and 1960s; *The Future of the Race* (Knopf, 1996), co-authored with Cornel West; and *Thirteen Ways of Looking at a Black Man* (Random House, 1997).

His honors and grants include a MacArthur Foundation "genius grant" (1981), the George Polk Award

for Social Commentary (1993), Chicago Tribune Heartland Award (1994), the Golden Plate Achievement Award (1995), *Time* magazine's "25 Most Influential Americans" list (1997), a National Humanities Medal (1998), and election to the American Academy of Arts and Letters (1999).

OPPOSITE, TOP ] *Colored People: A Memoir* (1994)

# FROM THE SOUL
Adapted from "Current Events," in *Colored People: A Memoir* (Knopf, 1994).

I entered the Davis Free Elementary School in Piedmont in 1956, just one year after it was integrated. There are many places where the integration of the schools lagged behind that of other social institutions. The opposite was true of Piedmont, and school was for many years after 1955 virtually our only integrated arena.

When I started at the "white school" (as we still thought of it), everybody I knew was excited about integration, and everybody was scared. In the newly integrated school system race was like an item of apparel that fitted us up all tight, like one of Mama's girdles. Nobody ever talked about race, but it was there in the lines drawn around socializing: colored go with colored, white with white, and we'll all get along. But even with such clear-cut rules, school was a fairly constant clash of cultures.

By the time I showed up at school, they were expecting me. Mama used to clean the houses of my teachers, Mrs. Mellor and Mrs. Bell, and they respected her. From the first day, I was marked out to excel. I was quiet, I was smart, I had a good memory, I already knew how to read and write, and I was blessed with the belief that I could learn anything. I was all set to become the little brown prince of that all-white school.

The teachers, in turn, pushed me and encouraged me. By second grade, it was entirely my world; there wasn't anything I couldn't learn. I loved the way Mrs. Mellor said my name Louis, as I was called. They gave me a test in the middle of the year, and I got 489 answers right out of 500. The other teachers had come down to Mrs. Mellor's room at the end of the hall and stared at the score sheet and then at me. These teachers were serious about learning, and about school. Piedmont had turned out most of the county's doctors. In a school of six grades and only 250 or so kids, that is quite something.

# Denise Giardina

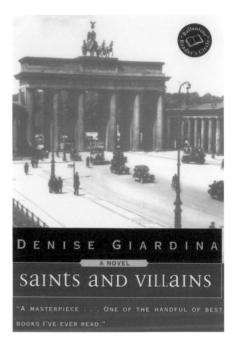

DENISE GIARDINA was born in Bluefield, West Virginia, in 1951. She grew up in the McDowell County coal camps of Black Wolf and Pageton. Her grandfather and uncles were coal miners. Her father, Dennis, who had come to America with his family from Sicily, became a coal company bookkeeper. Her mother, Leona, was from an eastern Kentucky farm family that had been in the Appalachian Mountains for generations. Leona became a nurse. Dennis and Leona had two children, Denise and her younger brother, Frank.

When Denise was thirteen, the local coal mine closed and many people, including her family, were forced to move away. They relocated in eastern Kanawha County, where Denise went to DuPont High School. She was active in a number of school activities, including the choir. She was also a Merit Scholarship Finalist. After high school, Denise attended West Virginia Wesleyan College, where she majored in history and minored in political science. She spent a semester abroad in England, where she began to research what would become her first novel, *Good King Harry*.

After graduation, Denise worked as a substitute teacher in the Kanawha County schools. Denise joined St. John's Episcopal Church in Charleston, and that spurred her interest in theology. She entered the Virginia Theological Seminary, an Episcopal seminary, in Alexandria, Virginia, and graduated in 1979.

While a student at Virginia Seminary, Denise joined a Christian community called Sojourners Fellowship in inner city Washington, D.C. Members of Sojourners held all their goods in common, in imitation of the early church, and lived a simple lifestyle on poverty-level incomes. Denise was involved with a number of community ministries, including a food co-op, daycare center, a Saturday youth program, tenant organizing and peace work.

From 1979-80, Denise returned to McDowell County for a year to work at an Episcopal Church in Northfork. There she organized the McDowell County

# HOMETOWN
## West Virginia

### BLACK WOLF

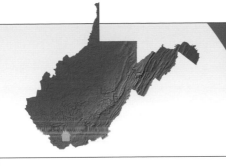

## FROM THE SOUL

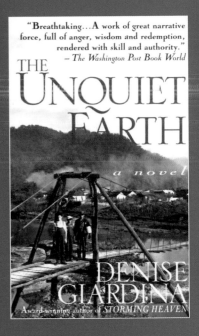

"Breathtaking...A work of great narrative force, full of anger, wisdom and redemption, rendered with skill and authority."
— *The Washington Post Book World*

**THE UNQUIET EARTH**

*a novel*

**DENISE GIARDINA**

Award-winning author of *STORMING HEAVEN*

---

portion of the Appalachian Land Ownership Study, a region-wide effort to catalog how much of Appalachia is owned by outside corporations and how much those corporations paid in taxes. Denise's research showed that over 80-percent of McDowell County is absentee-owned and that little is paid by the owners in taxes, contributing to the poverty of the county. Out of this research grew a number of community efforts and lawsuits. Denise returned to Sojourners and worked for the Episcopal Peace Fellowship. It was during this time she began writing her first novel, *Good King Harry*.

Giardina returned to West Virginia in 1982. *Good King Harry* was published in 1984. During this time, Denise worked first for Congressman Bob Wise, then for Secretary of State Ken Hechler. In 1986 she moved to eastern Kentucky and became an officer in Kentuckians for the Commonwealth, an activist group for strip mining and land ownership issues. Her third novel, *Storming Heaven*, was published a year later. Giardina moved to Durham, North Carolina, and wrote her next novel,

*The Unquiet Earth* – the sequel to *Storming Heaven*. Both books received the Weatherford Award for best books about the Appalachian South. *The Unquiet Earth* also won the Lillian Smith Award for Southern fiction. Giardina received the first of two fellowships from the National Endowment for the Arts.

In 1992, Denise Giardina returned to become Writer-in-Residence at West Virginia State College, later to become West Virginia State University. There she worked for six years to complete what she considers her best novel, *Saints and Villains*. This novel was named best book of the year by the Boston Book Review.

Denise Giardina continues to teach at West Virginia State University and has written *Fallam's Secret*, the first in a series about time travel.

---

OPPOSITE, TOP ] *Saints and Villains* (1998)

TOP, RIGHT ] *The Unquiet Earth* (1992)

---

My personal story in the public schools of West Virginia takes place in McDowell County and Kanawha County. I attended Thorpe Elementary School and Gary Junior High School, then DuPont Junior and Senior High Schools. In all four schools I found a sense of community. I was challenged by some good and caring teachers. And I found a sense of strength as I was forced to grow and face challenges along the way.

I was especially lucky to have excellent teachers all along the way – Miss Meade in first grade who challenged me to learn new words, Mrs. Altizer in fourth grade who fed my love of reading, Mrs. Resnick in seventh who introduced me to Shakespeare at an early age, Miss White and Mrs. Baroni in eighth and ninth who encouraged me to write stories and to read a wider variety of books, and Mrs. Hoffman in high school who turned her room into a book club at lunchtime.

I grew up among all sorts and conditions of people, and I learned that West Virginia was fertile ground for a fiction writer. It is ground I am still exploring, and I am proud to call it home.

*Denise Giardina*

# Homer Hickam

HOMER HICKAM, JR. was born on February 19, 1943, the second son of Homer and Elsie Hickam, and was raised in Coalwood, West Virginia. He graduated from Big Creek High School in 1960 and from the Virginia Polytechnic Institute (Virginia Tech) in 1964 with a B.S. in Industrial Engineering. A U.S. Army veteran, Mr. Hickam served as a First Lieutenant in the Fourth Infantry Division in Vietnam from 1967 to 1968 where he won the Army Commendation and Bronze Star medals. He served six years on active duty, leaving the service with the rank of Captain.

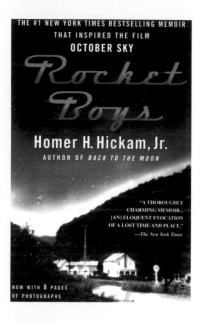

Hickam has been a writer since 1969 after his return from Vietnam. At first, he mostly wrote about his scuba diving adventures for a variety of different magazines. Then, after diving on many of the wrecks involved, he branched off into writing about the battle against the U-boats along the American east coast during World War II. This resulted in his first book, *Torpedo Junction* (1989), a military history best-seller published by the Naval Institute Press.

In 1998, Delacorte Press published Hickam's second book, *Rocket Boys: A Memoir*, the story of his life in the little town of Coalwood, West Virginia. It became an instant classic. *Rocket Boys* has since been translated into eight languages and also released as an abridged audio book and electronic book. Among its many honors, it was selected by the New York Times as one of its "Great Books of 1998" and was an alternate "Book-of-the-Month" selection for both the Literary Guild and Doubleday book clubs. *Rocket Boys* was also nominated by the National Book Critics Circle as Best Biography of 1998. In February, 1999, Universal Studios released its critically-acclaimed film *October Sky*, based on *Rocket Boys* (The title *October Sky* is an anagram of *Rocket Boys*). Delacorte subsequently released a mass market paperback of *Rocket Boys*, re-titled *October Sky. Rocket Boys/October Sky* reached the New York Times # 1 position on their best-seller list.

Mr. Hickam's first fiction novel was *Back to the Moon* (1999) and was simultaneously released as a hardcover, audio book, and eBook. It has also been translated into Chinese.

*The Coalwood Way* (2000), a memoir of Homer's hometown he calls "not a sequel but an equal," was published

# HOMETOWN
## West Virginia
### COALWOOD

# FROM THE SOUL

by Delacorte Press and is available in abridged audio, eBook, large print and Japanese. It was an alternate "Book-of-the-Month" selection for Doubleday's book club. His third Coalwood memoir, a true sequel, was published in October, 2001. It is titled *Sky of Stone* (2001). *Sky of Stone* is presently under development as a television movie. His final book about Coalwood was published in 2002, a self help/inspirational tome titled *We Are Not Afraid: Strength and Courage from the Town That Inspired the #1 Bestseller and Award-winning Movie October Sky.*

*The Keeper's Son* (2003), published by St. Martin's Press and set in the glorious Outer Banks of North Carolina during World War II, is the first of a series about Josh Thurlow, a Coast Guard officer, and his crew of misfits. The second novel in the series, the newly released *The Ambassador's Son* (2005), is set in the Solomon Islands of the South Pacific. It is anticipated that the third book in the series will be published in Spring 2006.

In all my travels, I am most heartened when I find teachers that remind me of the ones I had back in McDowell County, West Virginia. The teachers of the Coalwood School were as dedicated a bunch as ever existed. They believed that it was absolutely, utterly necessary to intensely teach us the basics of education – reading, writing, grammar, literature, and mathematics – without frills. When they observed a talent, they honed it as hard as they could until that talent shone like burnished gold. When they observed an educational weakness, they went after it like bobcats after a chipmunk. There was never any doubt that they were in charge of their classrooms, and if any of their students were so foolish as to question their authority, several layers of discipline were ready and willing to be applied, mostly notably by our parents. The teachers of Coalwood treated our education as serious and vital. They were convinced that their students were engaged in the most serious of enterprises. If we didn't learn, we would not succeed or prosper for the glory of the people who had raised us.

The teachers at Big Creek High School were similar to our Coalwood teachers. My physics and chemistry teacher in high school was Miss Freida Riley. Since my books *Rocket Boys* and *The Coalwood Way*, and also the movie *October Sky*, were released, Miss Riley has taken on near-icon status across the nation and the world. Wherever I go, I am thanked by people of all walks of life, but especially by tough teachers, for telling her story because they say it's their story, too. All of my teachers in West Virginia were tough because they needed to be. The results were dramatic. Most of my Coalwood classmates went on to college and nearly all of us succeeded at whatever we wanted to do with our lives.

*Homer Hickam*

OPPOSITE, LEFT ] *Rocket Boys: A Memoir (1998)*

TOP, RIGHT ] Hickam, with his father Homer Hickam, Sr., the day before shipping out to Vietnam.

# Kermit Hunter

## 1910-2001

The nation's most prolific writer of outdoor historical dramas, KERMIT HUNTER was born in Hallsville, West Virginia, on October 3, 1910. The son of Otis John and Lillian Farley Hunter, he began writing at an early age and, while still in high school, was a reporter and feature writer for his hometown newspaper. Always on the lookout for more to do, he also played piano and organ for silent movies.

After graduation from The Ohio State University, he attended the Julliard School of Music in New York City, followed by a tour of Europe playing piano concerts. But, in the mid-1930s, after receiving advice from a distinguished professor of music to go home and practice piano for seven more years, he returned to West Virginia to assist in trading minor league baseball players for the Mountain State League.

At the outbreak of World War II, Hunter enlisted in the National Guard and, within three years, was on the general staff of the Pentagon. Later, from a position in Panama, he planned the American defense of the Caribbean, for which he won the Legion of Merit.

He left the service as a lieutenant colonel and accepted a position as business manager for the North Carolina Symphony in Raleigh. At the same time, 1949, he worked on a Master's degree in dramatic art at the University of North Carolina at Chapel Hill, where he wrote the outdoor drama *Unto These Hills* as his thesis. The drama, first produced in 1950, was about the removal of

## HOMETOWN
### West Virginia

HALLSVILLE

# OUTDOOR DRAMAS

Cherokee Indians from North Carolina to Oklahoma and went on to become the second oldest outdoor drama in the nation, playing to more than 14 million people by the time of his death.

Caught up in the university atmosphere at Chapel Hill, he also went on to earn a Ph.D. in English Literature.

After a year as a Guggenheim Fellow spent in writing, Hunter accepted a position at Hollins College in Roanoke, Virginia, in the drama department and as chairman of the Fine Arts Department in 1964. He went on to become the dean of the Meadows School of the Arts and at Southern Methodist University in Dallas, Texas.

An early practitioner of site-specific drama, writing plays to be staged in a given location, Hunter wrote over 40 outdoor dramas for many communities across the United States. All of them were fashioned with historical themes and uplifting values. *Horn in the West*, a story of the American Revolution and

Appalachian frontiersman Daniel Boone, has been performed in Boone, North Carolina, since 1952. Hunter's *Honey in the Rock* has been performed in Beckley, West Virginia, since 1959. This legacy earned him the title of "Dean of Outdoor Drama Playwrights."

In recognition for his contributions to American drama, both Emory and Henry College and Oklahoma Christian College awarded Kermit Hunter honorary doctorates. From 1978 to 1993, Hunter held the position of senior lecturer at the University of Texas, Arlington. Kermit Hunter died on April 11, 2001 in Dallas, Texas.

OPPOSITE, INSET ] *Unto These Hills* program (2004).

OPPOSITE, TOP ] Scene from *Unto These Hills.*

TOP, RIGHT ] Scene from *Horn in the West.*

| | |
|---|---|
| *The Heart of a City* | *Daniel Shay's Rebellion* |
| *That Untraveled World* | *Honey in the Rock* |
| *Trail of Tears* | *The Burning Hour* |
| *McIntosh Trail* | *Dawn of Promise* |
| *Wings of the Morning* | *This Mighty Struggle* |
| *The Mistress of the Inn* | *Thy Kingdom Come* |
| *Homecoming in Magdala* | *Unto These Hills* |
| *Thunder on the River* | *The Home Road* |
| *Eleventh Hour* | *Voice in the Wind* |
| *Next Day in the Morning* | *Beyond the Sundown* |
| *The Bell and the Plow* | *Bound for Kentucky* |
| *Forever This Land* | *Chucky Jack* |
| *Bright Hope* | *Hernando de Soto* |
| *The Third Frontier* | *The Liberty Tree* |
| *Walk Toward the Sunset* | *Horn in the West* |
| *The Golden Land* | *The Golden Crucible* |
| *The Golden Prairie* | *Stars in My Crown* |
| *Dust on Her Petticoats* | *Come Sing Tomorrow* |

# McKinney
### Irene

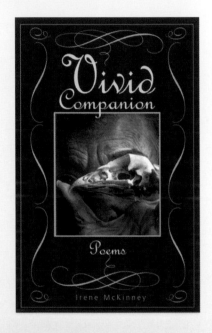

IRENE MCKINNEY grew up on a farm in Barbour County, West Virginia. She learned to read at age three and has continued to be an avid reader. She attended a one-room school, Concord School, for her first five grades and received a double promotion from the second grade to the fourth grade. She then began her sixth grade year at Belington Grade School and later attended Belington High School, where she graduated in 1956.

Photo: Kate Long

Her life on the farm, as well as her reading of the classic poets, influenced her desire to write. She began writing poems and stories at the age of ten, and studied poetry and literature with a sustained interest and zeal.

She married shortly after her graduation from high school and is the mother of two children, a daughter, Julia, and a son, Paul. She divorced her husband in 1974.

McKinney received her B.A. from West Virginia Wesleyan College, her M.A. from West Virginia University, where she submitted a creative thesis, and her Ph.D. from the University of Utah, where her dissertation was a volume of poetry.

She began publishing her work in the late 1960s and early 1970s and has continued to publish in prominent journals around the country, as well as in collections and anthologies. She has published five collections of poetry and has edited a volume of West Virginia writers. Recent poems appear in *The American Voice, Artful Dodge, The Kenyon Review, Confluence, The Georgia Review, Poetry Northwest,*

*Northwest Review, Kestrel, Poetry* and many others. Over three hundred of McKinney's poems have appeared in journals and magazines.

She has been writer-in-residence at a number of colleges and universities, including the University of California at Santa Cruz, Western Washington University at Bellingham and the University of New Mexico in

## HOMETOWN
**West Virginia**

BELINGTON

*West Virginia, where the hills are flung around like old green handkerchiefs and the Chessie rumbles along, shaking the smooth clean skin of the river.*

Albuquerque.  She has held regular academic positions at Hamilton College, Potomac State College and West Virginia Wesleyan College. She was appointed Poet Laureate of West Virginia in 1994.

Irene McKinney lives in a small house near the woods on the edge of her family's farm in Barbour County.

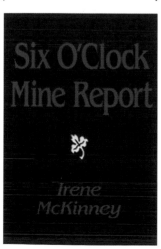

OPPOSITE, LEFT ] *Vivid Companion* (2004)

LEFT ] *Six O'Clock Mine Report* (1989)

## FROM THE SOUL

I was fortunate to grow up where and when I did.  I went to a one-room school where there were only 30 students in five grades, and I listened and learned not only from the teacher but from classmates in higher grades reading aloud and being instructed.  My teacher, Mrs. Teeter, recognized that I was a precocious reader, and she encouraged me and gave me a "double promotion," which made me realize that I had ability.

In high school, Leah Richards, a bright, enthusiastic English teacher, gave me further encouragement by recognizing my poetry writing.  One of my poems was nominated by my teachers for a statewide anthology – that was my very first publication, and it helped set me on the course of being a writer.

Even though I was an eccentric, difficult child, two or three teachers along the way encouraged and helped me.  When people say this state is backward, I simply am astounded.  I had access to a farm community, a small peaceful town and school and good, dedicated teachers.  I was in nature and in literature – a perfect combination for a writer.

*Irene McKinney*

# Louise McNeill

## 1911-1993

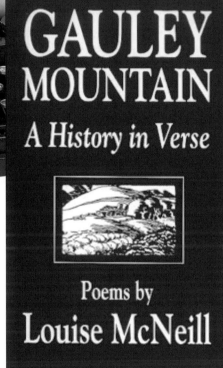

**GAULEY MOUNTAIN**
*A History in Verse*

Poems by
**Louise McNeill**

Former West Virginia Poet Laureate Louise McNeill grew up on a rocky farm in Pocahontas County. She was born at Buckeye in 1911 and began teaching in local one-room schools in 1930, at age 19. After seven years in rural education, Louise McNeill taught at Aiken Preparatory School in South Carolina from 1941 to 1946.

College teaching brought McNeill back home to West Virginia when she returned to an assistant professorship at West Virginia University in 1948. She later taught at Potomac State College, Concord College and Fairmont State, where she was professor of history from 1969 until her retirement in 1973.

McNeill earned a B.A. from Concord College and an M.A. at Miami of Ohio. She attended the Bread Loaf School of English in Vermont, where she worked with Robert Frost, and the University of Iowa's writers' workshop. McNeill also holds a Ph.D. in history and English from West Virginia University.

Also known by her married name, Louise McNeill Pease, the distinguished poet was named West Virginian of the Year in 1985. She was active in various

# HOMETOWN
## West Virginia

### BUCKEYE

*Despite substantial literary and scholarly achievements, Louise McNeill listed "farm background" at the top of her résumé. Her writing evokes universal feelings, but the subtleties and language of West Virginia predominate.*

Appalachian festivals, writers' workshops and official events in her capacity as poet laureate. She has appeared at Mountain State colleges, on educational television and on radio programs.

Despite substantial literary and scholarly achievements, Louise McNeill listed "farm background" at the top of her résumé. Her writing

OPPOSITE, TOP ] *Gauley Mountain* (1939)

THIS PAGE, RIGHT ] McNeill's high school photo (1927).

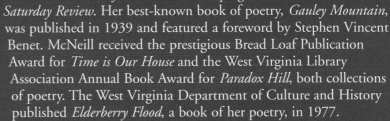

evokes universal feelings, but the subtleties and language of rural West Virginia predominate.

Her publications include books of poetry; prose, fiction and essays; scholarly works; contractions to anthologies and textbooks; and poetry published in periodicals from *Harpers* and *Atlantic Monthly* to *Good Housekeeping* and *Saturday Review*. Her best-known book of poetry, *Gauley Mountain*, was published in 1939 and featured a foreword by Stephen Vincent Benet. McNeill received the prestigious Bread Loaf Publication Award for *Time is Our House* and the West Virginia Library Association Annual Book Award for *Paradox Hill*, both collections of poetry. The West Virginia Department of Culture and History published *Elderberry Flood*, a book of her poetry, in 1977.

With *The Milkweed Ladies*, her 1988 prose memoir, Louise McNeill returned once again to her beloved theme of life in the mountains. Through these stories of one West Virginia family, she touched us all with a longing for simpler and sweeter times.

Louise McNeill provided a colorfully lyrical way of looking into West Virginia's past. After the reissue of Gauley Mountain in 1989, the publication of *Hill Daughter: New and Selected Poems* in 1991 and a 1991 radio version of *Gauley Mountain*, Louise McNeill Pease died in June of 1993.

[Courtesy www.gauleymountain.org]

# Jayne Anne Phillips

JAYNE ANNE PHILLIPS was born and raised in West Virginia. Her first book of stories, *Black Tickets,* published in 1979, won the prestigious Sue Kaufman Prize for First Fiction, awarded by the American Academy and Institute of Arts and Letters. Featured in Newsweek, *Black Tickets* was pronounced "stories unlike any in our literature – a crooked beauty" by Raymond Carver and established Phillips as a writer "in love with the American language."

She was praised by Nadine Gordimer as "the best short story writer since Eudora Welty," and *Black Tickets* has since become a classic of the short story genre.

*Machine Dreams*, Phillips' first novel, published in 1984, observes one American family from the turn of the century through the Vietnam War. A New York Times best seller, *Machine Dreams* was nominated for the National Book Critics Circle Award and chosen by the New York Times Book Review as one of twelve "Best Books of the Year." Her book of stories, *Fast Lanes* (1987), praised in the *LA Times* as "stories that hover on the edge of poetry," was re-issued by Vintage in 2001 with three previously uncollected stories.

*Shelter* (1994), a haunting evocation of childhood rite-of-passage, was awarded an Academy Award in Literature by the American Academy and Institute of Arts and Letters and chosen one of the "Best Books of the Year" by Publishers Weekly.

*Motherkind* (2000), published by Knopf, examines timeless questions of birth and death. *Motherkind* won the Massachusetts Book Award and was nominated for Britain's Orange Prize. Phillips' works are published in twelve languages.

She is the recipient of a Guggenheim Fellowship, two National Endowment for the Arts Fellowships, a Bunting Fellowship and a 2004 Howard Foundation Fellowship. Her work has appeared most recently in *Harper's*,

## HOMETOWN
### West Virginia

BUCKHANNON

*Granta, Doubletake,* and the *Norton Anthology of Contemporary Fiction.* She has taught at Harvard University, Williams College and Boston University, and is currently Writer-In-Residence at Brandeis University. New work is forthcoming in *Tin House* and *Granta.*

Up-to-date information, including essays, can be viewed at:

www.JayneAnnePhillips.com

---

OPPOSITE, LEFT ] *Black Tickets* (1979)

TOP, RIGHT ] *Motherkind* (2000)

BOTTOM, RIGHT ] *Machine Dreams* (1984)

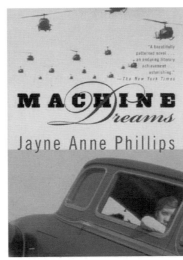

# FROM THE SOUL

What I remember most about my seventeen years of public education in West Virginia is how well my best teachers taught, despite a paucity of support or resources. I remember my 1959 first grade class at Academy Grade School in Buckhannon as including fifty children. Surely this memory is incorrect, but there were certainly thirty-five or forty of us, and at least one of us (me) turned out to be a compulsive reader. "Music class" throughout the grades consisted of singing folk songs in the morning before loudspeaker announcements, and the beautiful words and haunting melodies of songs like *Charming Billy* and *She'll Be Coming Around the Mountain* later made their appearance in my novels.

By some stroke of incredible luck, Irene McKinney was my ninth grade "student teacher" in English at Buckhannon Upshur High School. I didn't know Irene was an accomplished poet, or that she would become a valued mentor, friend and colleague years later. Her example has sustained me all my life, but our first "discussion" of writing took place in the temporary outbuilding in which freshmen labored over the sentence diagrams I detested, and the less frequently encouraged "creative essays." I'd stayed after class to receive from Irene's hands an essay I'd written about the ocean. It was, I'm sure, jam-packed with adjectives, but Irene saw something in it. "People will try to bury you," she said to me, "but you mustn't let them." The recognition implicit in her statement struck me like the proverbial lightning bolt. I sensed already that life, particularly in West Virginia, was lyrically beautiful and darkly layered, that truth was complex, that writers knew this perhaps too deeply, that knowing too much makes people vulnerable, and that knowledge is risky. Irene's words assured me that language and the creation of language were powerful enough to defy any discouragement, and I took her words to heart.

I wish every student in West Virginia the gift and armor of literature, and the exquisite risk of writing it.

# Beverly Van Hook

BEVERLY HENNEN VAN HOOK, author of the beloved *Supergranny* children's mystery series and the *Liza and Dutch* mysteries for adults, was born and grew up in Huntington, West Virginia.

"I decided to be a writer when I was about ten years old," she said. "Until then I'd planned to be a firefighter, a career goal ever since my Vacation Bible School class had visited the Guyandotte fire station. But I always loved to read and at ten I read Louisa May Alcott's *Little Women* and – boom – I had to be a writer like Jo.

"When I was about thirteen someone told me about this thing called 'journalism' where they paid you MONEY to write. Wow, what a concept, I thought, and set my sights on studying journalism at Ohio University, Athens."

Bev graduated from Huntington High School where she was president of the National Honor Society and Honorarian commencement speaker. With the unflagging encouragement of her family, the help of summer jobs (at *The Point Pleasant Register* and as a stringer for *The Charleston Daily Mail*), a scholarship and a board job, she became the first college graduate in her family.

She was graduated from Ohio University in 1962 and worked as a journalist for 22 years, editing company publications, reporting for newspapers and writing freelance articles for numerous magazines including *Reader's Digest*, *Family Circle* and *The Lion*. In 1963 she married fellow Ohio University graduate Don Van Hook. The couple had three children and lived for many years in the Midwest and Europe.

In 1985 she turned to fiction, beginning her *Supergranny* children's mysteries about a gray-haired detective who drives a red Ferrari and fights crime. The first book, *The Mystery of the Shrunken Heads*, sold out in ten months and has gone into five printings. With the second case, *Supergranny* received her first national review in School Library Journal and a recommendation by the Parents Committee of the Illinois Reading Association.

The *Supergranny* crime-fighting team includes her spoiled mini-robot, Chesterton, and the three children next door, loosely based on Bev's own

## HOMETOWN
### West Virginia

### HUNTINGTON

## FROM THE SOUL

*"The beauty of the hills still makes my heart leap. West Virginia is a place of infinite fascination."*

three kids when they were that age. "Shackleford, the bashful Old English Sheepdog, is the only absolutely real character in the book," Bev says. "She was our dog down to the paws; I just changed her name to protect her privacy."

In addition to writing, Bev has been a frequent speaker at schools and libraries throughout the United States and has returned to West Virginia many times to conduct writing workshops and to speak at the West Virginia Reading Association's conference at the Greenbrier.

After her husband took early retirement from his job as an advertising executive for Deere & Company, the couple moved from Illinois to Charlottesville, Virginia, to be closer to family, and Bev now has

fun reading *Supergranny* books with her own three grandchildren.

Her first adult mystery, *Fiction, Fact, & Murder*, was set in West Virginia, and her second, *Juliet's Ghost*, published in 2003, has scenes in the state as well.

"My family, teachers and friends in West Virginia read to me and with me, inspired and encouraged me; I'll never forget them. The beauty of the hills still makes my heart leap. West Virginia is a place of infinite fascination."

OPPOSITE, LEFT ] Bev with husband, Don, at book signing.

TOP, RIGHT ] Bev with "Shackleford."

West Virginia is the place above all others that shaped me and my work. Not only is it where I was born and grew up, it's where I learned to read standing behind my father's chair, following his moving finger as he read the funnies aloud. It's where my grandmother read Birds' *Christmas Carol* and *The Five Little Peppers* to me and where Jane Ann Garrett in Guyandotte, a girl so incredibly rich that she owned every Nancy Drew book, was so incredibly generous that she loaned them all to me. And it's where, after I decided to be a writer, my mother bought me a used typewriter out of her grocery money at two dollars per week.

When I graduated from Huntington High School in 1958 I was a Merit Scholarship semi-finalist, which said much more about my teachers than it said about me, as we had eleven semi-finalists that year.

My dedicated teachers whetted my curiosity to learn everything I could and made it abundantly clear they expected me to keep at it forever. It was here that I got the notions never to put on airs, that all people are equal, that much in life is beautiful and good, and that loyalty is a commandment.

I still spend many weeks each year in West Virginia, and my heart still leaps at its majestic beauty. My fervent prayer is that its beauty will be protected and its people, all of them, will prosper.

*Bev Van Hook*

# Patrick Boyd

PATRICK BOYD grew up in the coalfields of McDowell County and graduated from Northfork High School in 1983. Although an avid fan of the basketball empire helmed by his late father, Coach Jennings Boyd, sports was not to be his destiny.

Patrick enrolled at West Virginia University to pursue a career in musical theatre and further his skills as a professional magician. While training at WVU, he performed in numerous stage productions (including a summer season at Theatre West Virginia in Beckley, West Virginia) and was requested by the university president to perform his amazing legerdemain at several black tie functions. Patrick transferred to East Carolina University to finish his education and graduated Magna Cum Laude in 1988 with degrees in Theatre Arts and Dance.

Now a resident of New York City since 1990, Patrick's illustrious career has spanned Broadway, film and television, appearances on *The Tonight Show*, *The Tony Awards* and cabaret stages around the world.

Patrick could be seen starring as Bobby Child in the Tony Award-winning musical *Crazy For You* in Basel, Switzerland, to sell-out crowds. Prior to that, he performed the role for eight months in Hamburg, Munich and Berlin and in the Broadway National Tour to critical acclaim.

His Broadway credits include the original revival company and cast recording of Tommy Tune's *Grease!*, starring Rosie O'Donnell and later Brooke Shields, and the role of the Tin Man in *The Wizard of Oz*, starring Roseanne. Off-Broadway, Patrick was featured in the hit musical revue, *Naked Boys Singing*.

In 1993, Patrick was thrilled to work side-by-side with his favorite icon, Bette Midler, in the Emmy Award-winning CBS move *Gypsy* – the first ever TV film

## HOMETOWN
### Westerville Virginia
### NORTHFORK

# FROM THE SOUL

Finding an outlet for creative expression at a high school known for its athletic prowess wasn't easy. After all, my father had coached the Blue Demons of Northfork High School to eight consecutive state championships in basketball, an unprecedented feat in high school sports. Nonetheless, there was an occasional magician or theatre troupe that would set up shop in our gymnasium, and those were exciting days for me. I found the presentations to be fascinating, as we had no drama department or school plays.

I did participate, however, in various talent shows, fashion shows and skits presented to the student body under the guidance of a wonderful faculty member, Scarlett Goosens. She knew the importance of integrating these types of activities, even on a shoestring budget, into our regular academic routine. These shows challenged us to be creative, spontaneous and more than likely laid the groundwork for what would eventually become, for me, a career in theatre.

*Patrick Boyd*

of a Broadway musical. Other notable collaborations include work with Kim Zimmer (from *The Guiding Light*), Jason Alexander, Martin Short, Alan Ruck, Ann B. Davis and Maureen McCormick (both of Brady Bunch fame), Mickey Dolenz, Andrea Martin, Eddie Bracken and Bob Mackie.

Patrick recently returned to New York after traveling for over a year in the national tour of the hit Broadway musical *The Producers*, performing the lead roles of Leo Bloom and the campy Carmen Ghia. He can be seen in the upcoming film version of *The*

*Producers*, starring Nathan Lane, Matthew Broderick and Uma Thurman, in theaters December of 2005.

---

OPPOSITE, TOP ] (l-r) Boyd with Peter Riegert and Bette Midler during the filming of *Gypsy* (1993); with Brooke Shields on the set of *Grease!* (1994).

ABOVE ] Boyd as Leo Bloom in *The Producers* (2004).

TOP, RIGHT ] *Singin' in the Rain* at the Merry-Go-Round Playhouse (2003).

# Ted Cassidy

### 1932-1979

Born in Pittsburgh and raised in Philippi, West Virginia, THEODORE "TED" CASSIDY reached great heights in life, both as a man and as an actor.

An unusually bright child, Cassidy was in the third grade by the time he was six years old. This alone was enough to set Cassidy apart from his classmates, but there was something else that made him *different*. By the time he was an eleven-year-old high school freshman, he was six feet-one inch tall. Eventually reaching six feet-nine, he was a natural for Philippi High School's football and basketball teams.

Developing an interest in dramatics while attending college at West Virginia Wesleyan, then Stetson University, where he played one successful season of college basketball, Cassidy went out of his way to play characters of all physical types and sizes; he may well have been the tallest Falstaff in theatrical history. Though offered a singing job with the Paul Whiteman Orchestra, he decided on a career as a radio announcer. Working for WFAA radio in Dallas, Texas, he covered John F. Kennedy's assassination and was one of the firsts to interview eyewitnesses.

Within a year, Cassidy moved to California to seriously pursue an acting career and ended up landing the first role for which he auditioned: Lurch, the lumbering, monosyllabic butler on the TV comedy series *The Addams Family*. The role of Lurch was supposed to be a silent one, as in the Charles Addams cartoons. However, during the shooting of the pilot, when Ted made his very first appearance at the sounding of the gong, he ad libbed – in his trademark sonorous voice – the now famous line, "You rang?" Everyone was so impressed that Lurch became a speaking role.

Photo: Don Cravens/Time Life Pictures/Getty Images

Snap! Snap!

## HOMETOWN
■ West Virginia ■

PHILIPPI

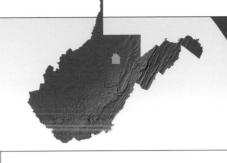

# "You rang?"

He went on to provide the voice and physical model for Injun Joe on *The New Adventures of Huck Finn*, a 1968 animation/live-action hybrid produced by Hanna-Barbera. He also supplied the voice of "The Thing" on Hanna-Barbera's Saturday morning cartoon series *The New Fantastic Four*, a funny coincidence since he also played the disembodied hand "Thing" on *The Addams Family*. Cassidy's deep voice was frequently used in animated series, including *Scooby Doo, Where Are You?* and *Space Ghost*, and he could be heard as the narrator during the opening credits of TV's *The Incredible Hulk*.

Though limited in his choice of screen roles, he shared the big screen with Paul Newman and Robert Redford as the outlaw Harvey Logan in 1969's *Butch Cassidy and the Sundance Kid*. Cassidy continued to play small television parts well into the 1970s, including appearances on *I Dream of Jeannie*, *Star Trek*, *Bonanza* and *The Six Million Dollar Man*.

In 1979, at the age of 46, Ted Cassidy passed away from complications following heart surgery.

OPPOSITE ] Ted Cassidy as Lurch during scene from *The Addams Family*.

## THE ADDAMS FAMILY

They're creepy and they're kookey.

Mysterious and spookey.

They're altogether ookey.

The Addams Family.

The house is a museum.

When people come to see'em.

They really are a scre-am.

The Addams Family.

Neat. Sweet. Petite.

So get a witch's shawl on.

A broomstick you can crawl on.

We're going to pay a call on.

The Addams Family.

–Vic Mizzy

# Michael Cerveris

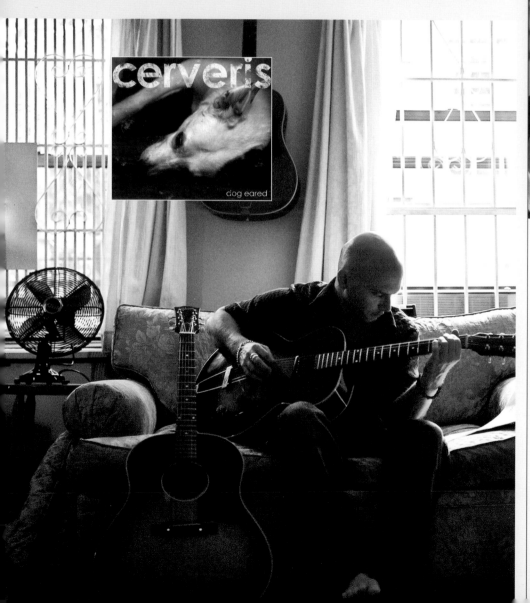

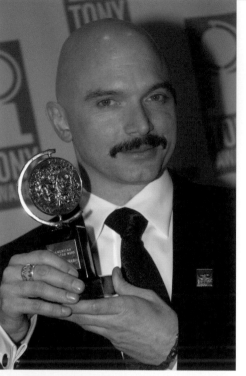

MICHAEL CERVERIS' multifaceted career as actor, musician, singer and songwriter spans the disparate worlds of dramatic theater, indie/alternative rock and Broadway musicals, as well as work in television and film. On Broadway, he received a Tony Award and an Outer Critics Circle Award for his portrayal of John Wilkes Booth in *Assassins* – which also received a Grammy nomination for original cast recording.

Other Broadway appearances include originating the title role in *The Who's Tommy* (Tony nomination, Theater World Award, Original Cast Grammy) and *Titanic, The Musical.* On London's West End he starred in *Hedwig and the Angry Inch* – a role he also performed off-Broadway and in Los Angeles (Garland Award, Ovation Award nomination). Other off-Broadway appearances include Charles L. Mee's *Wintertime*, revivals of *Fifth of July* and *Total Eclipse*, Maria Irene Fornes' *Abingdon Square* (premiere) and *The Games* with Meredith Monk and Ping Chong (BAM Next Wave). He made his Lincoln Center debut with Duncan Sheik in a concert version of *Spring Awakening* for the American Songbook series and also starred there in *Passion,* which was broadcast on PBS' *Live From Lincoln Center* series. In theaters across the country he has been seen as Romeo (Goodman, Old Globe), Puck (Dallas Theater Center), Crow in *Tooth of Crime* (Hartford Stage), Duke of Aumerle in *Richard II* (Mark Taper Forum), Claudio in *Measure for Measure* (Old Globe), Don John in *Much Ado About Nothing* (La Jolla), Giorgio in *Passion* (Kennedy Center,  Ravinia Festival, Friends In Deed benefit on Broadway), George in *Sunday In The Park With George* (Ravinia Festival) and Carl Magnus in *A Little Night Music* (Chicago Shakespeare Theater, Jefferson award nomination).  This summer Michael will again join Lonny Price, Patti Lupone and Audra MacDonald for a third consecutive year at

# HOMETOWN
## West Virginia

### HUNTINGTON

## FROM THE SOUL

Ravinia in *Anyone Can Whistle*. Notable film appearances include *The Mexican* opposite Julia Roberts and James Gandolfini, *Rock And Roll High School Forever*, Paul Auster's *Lulu on the Bridge* and *Tokyo Pop*. Mr. Cerveris was a regular on the television series *Fame* and *The American Embassy*, and guest starred on the first season finale of *CSI*, *Dr. Vegas* with Rob Lowe, *The Equalizer* and many others.

As a musician, he toured the US & UK as guitarist with punk icon Bob Mould (of the bands Husker Du and Sugar). He also toured with Pete Townshend, sang with The Breeders

and Stone Temple Pilots and opened for Frank Black (The Pixies) and Lloyd Cole. He was invited to speak at the Rock and Roll Hall of Fame as part of an exhibition celebrating the history of The Who and Tommy. As Hedwig, he supported Boy George and Culture Club at Radio City Music Hall on New Year's Eve 1999. His recent debut solo album, *Dog Eared* (Low Heat Records), includes guest appearances by Laura Cantrell and members of Sonic Youth, Teenage Fanclub, Guided By Voices, Sleater-Kinney, Varnaline and The Posies. He is next scheduled to star on Broadway in the title role of *Sweeney Todd* in that show's upcoming revival.

OPPOSITE, INSET] *Dog Eared* (2004)

OPPOSITE, TOP] Michael with his Tony Award for *Assassins*.

LEFT] Performance in *Passion* at Lincoln Center.

TOP, RIGHT] On tour with Bob Mould.

Looking back on my unpredictable and sometimes outright strange career over the years, I'm not sure the West Virginia public school system will want to take credit for having given me some early tools for my life in the arts. After all, between wearing dresses, toting guns, deafening mosh pits and sinking ocean liners, I'm maybe not a shining example for the youth of the wild, wonderful state I claim as my boyhood home. But for better or worse, it was there, while my father taught piano at Marshall University and my mother taught dance and raised three kids in Huntington, that I had teachers like Irvine Parsons at Beverly Hills Jr. High. Not content with teaching my classmates and me the finer points of glee club singing, Ms. Parsons had the foresight and gumption (or recklessness) to start a class in "Rock Band." Using music that we loved as a gateway, a handful of us met in the music room several hours each week and developed our skills, enhanced our appreciation of the rudiments of music and annoyed neighboring classrooms as we set out to learn enough songs to play for our unlucky fellow students at the Valentine's Day Dance and assorted Sock Hops (yes, we actually called them that). But what I learned most of all from teachers like Ms. Parsons and the many music, literature and visual arts classes I had in my public school years in West Virginia were fundamental skills of collaboration, integration, synthesis and creative problem solving that have benefited me in every aspect of my life on and off stage. And even more importantly, it encouraged my appreciation for the creations of beauty that centuries of artists have crafted to break down barriers, elevate the minds and open the hearts of their fellow men and women. I can think of no more valuable lessons in these troubling and uncertain times.

# Paul Dooley

The year 1977 was a big one for actor PAUL DOOLEY. That's when he was "discovered," and after 25 years in show business, became an overnight success.

It all happened when legendary film director Robert Altman caught him on stage in the Jules Feiffer comedy *Hold Me*. Altman, who had achieved fame with *M\*A\*S\*H* and *Nashville*, signed Dooley on the spot to play Carol Burnett's husband in his upcoming film *A Wedding*.

After another starring role in Altman's *A Perfect Couple*, Paul landed the part that would change his life forever in the coming-of-age classic *Breaking Away*.

His hilarious portrayal of the long-suffering Dad earned him critical acclaim, and set the stage for another triumph, in the beloved John Hughes comedy *Sixteen Candles*. As Molly Ringwald's distracted yet sympathetic father, Dooley endeared himself to an entire generation of young people.

Since then, he's played the father of some of our finest actresses, including Helen Hunt, Toni Collette, Mia Farrow and Julia Roberts (in *Runaway Bride*). In addition to being Hollywood's favorite Dad, Dooley has become one of the busiest actors working today, creating one memorable character

Photo: Diana Michener

## HOMETOWN
### West Virginia

#### PARKERSBURG

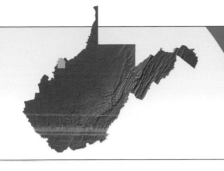

## FROM THE SOUL

after another in such films as *Popeye*, with Robin Williams, where he appeared as the hamburger-loving Wimpy; a part, Dooley says, that he played with relish. Other films include *Paternity*, with Burt Reynolds, *Kiss Me Goodbye*, opposite Sally Field and Jeff Bridges, *Happy Texas*, with William H. Macy, *Insomnia*, with Al Pacino and *Waiting for Guffman* and *A Mighty Wind*, both with Christopher Guest.

On the small screen, Dooley starred in his own sitcom, *Coming Of Age*, on CBS, which kicked off a series of recurring roles on other TV shows, including *E.R.*, *Grace Under Fire*, *My So-Called Life*, *Star Trek: Deep Space Nine*, *Once And Again*, *Curb Your Enthusiasm*, HBO's *Dream On*, for which he received an Emmy Nomination, and a feisty judge on *The Practice*, for which he received his second Emmy Nomination.

Upon graduation from West Virginia University, Paul headed for New York City with just fifty dollars in his pocket. To pay the rent, he worked as a clown, entertaining kids with his magic and juggling skills. Luckily one of his college chums was none other than Don Knotts. Already a working actor, Knotts helped Paul land his first role on TV, playing a comic cowboy.

After a few years as a nightclub comic, he landed on *The Tonight Show*. From there he joined Second City, the famous improvisational troupe.  Next stop: Broadway! Paul was cast in the original company of *The Odd Couple*.

Paul lives in Los Angeles with one of his favorite writers, Winnie Holzman (also his wife). She is the creator of the highly acclaimed television series *My So-Called Life* and most recently the Broadway musical *Wicked*, with songs by Stephen Schwartz of *Godspell* fame. He is the real-life father of four children: Robin, Adam, Peter and Savannah; and the proud grandfather of three.

OPPOSITE, BOTTOM] Dooley as Wimpy in *Popeye* (1980).

OPPOSITE, TOP] Dooley with Al Pacino and Hilary Swank in *Insomnia* (2002).

I had a huge crush on my third grade teacher. Her name was Miss Knotts, and she was beautiful. This was at Neale school in Vienna, West Virginia, and Miss Knotts inspired me. I wrote a poem which she liked well enough to have printed in the school paper – my first taste of celebrity. This is how the poem began:

*Oh, you little golden rod / You're such a funny fellow*
*With your little stem of brown / And little cap of yellow*

I had a lot of other teachers at Neale who meant a lot to me, but none more than my homeroom teacher. She was very maternal and treated her students almost like family.

Another teacher, who had a particular influence on me, was Eva Wells, who taught English. She introduced her eighth graders to literature by acting out the characters in the stories and bringing them excitingly to life.

In grade school I was always drawing – usually very realistic pictures of cars and planes. When I went to Parkersburg High School I discovered cartooning and gave up my cars and planes for a world of funny faces.

My art teacher encouraged me to pursue my new passion. She allowed me to work on my cartoons while everyone else was drawing bowls of fruit. My reward was becoming the staff cartoonist on the school paper – one of the thrills of my life.

Another ambition of mine was to become an actor. Luckily for me there was Edith Humphrey, the drama teacher, who nurtured and supported my talent through a number of school plays. She knew many of the secrets to good acting, and lessons I learned from her I still use to this day.

*Paul Dooley*

# Brad Dourif

A veteran of both stage and film, BRAD DOURIF continues to make a lasting impression on American culture. Dourif began his career in theater but received worldwide critical acclaim for his motion picture performance in *One Flew Over the Cuckoo's Nest*.

His performance was recognized with one of film community's highest honors – an Academy Award nomination in 1975. In addition to the Academy nomination, the Hollywood Foreign Press Association honored Brad with the 1977 Golden Globe Award for Best Newcomer. Most recently, he earned an Emmy nomination for his portrayal as 'the Doctor' on the critically-acclaimed HBO series *Deadwood*.

Born and raised in Huntington, West Virginia, Brad started acting in school productions and progressed to community theater, joining up with the Huntington Community Players while attending Marshall University of Huntington. At age 19, he relocated to New York City where he worked with the Circle Repertory Company. During the early 1970s, Dourif appeared in a number of plays, off-Broadway and at Woodstock, New York, including *The Ghost Sonata, The Doctor in Spite of Himself* and *When You Comin' Back, Red Rider?* in which he was spotted by director Milos Forman who cast him in *One Flew Over the Cuckoo's Nest*.

A true character actor, Brad's intensity has found him playing a diverse range of characters in numerous films such as *Eyes of Laura Mars*, John Huston's *Wise Blood* and Milos Forman's *Ragtime*. Dourif also teamed up with director David Lynch for *Dune* and *Blue Velvet*. His broad skill set also served him well in a number of horror films, notably as the voice of the evil doll Chucky in *Child's Play* and its sequels.

Since his television debut in the PBS film *The Mound Builders*, Dourif has also made appearances in a number of television series, such as *The X Files, Babylon 5, Star Trek: Voyager* and *Ponderosa*.

## HOMETOWN
### West Virginia

HUNTINGTON

*"Why indeed should we welcome you,
Master Stormcrow? Lathspell I name you!
Ill news; and ill news is an ill guest they say."*

–Grima Wormtongue, *The Lord of the Rings*

Dourif's recent film work includes the role of Grima Wormtongue in Peter Jackson's epic trilogy *The Lord of the Rings.*

Brad makes his home in Los Angeles, California.

OPPOSITE, LEFT ] Dourif as Doc on the HBO series *Deadwood.*

LEFT ] On the cover of *Huntington Quarterly* (Spring 2003).

Courtesy of HQ Publishing

# FILMOGRAPHY

*Seed of Chucky* (2004), Voice of Chucky

*The Lord of the Rings: The Return of the King* (2003), Grima Wormtongue

*The Lord of the Rings: The Two Towers* (2002), Grima Wormtongue

*Bride of Chucky* (1998), Voice of Chucky

*Alien: Resurrection* (1997), Dr. Jonathan Gediman

*Color of Night* (1994), Clark

*Amos & Andrew* (1993), Officer Donnie Donaldson

*Final Judgement* (1992), Father Tyrone

*Child's Play 3* (1991), Voice of Chucky

*Jungle Fever* (1991), Leslie

*Child's Play 2* (1990) (voice), Voice of Chucky

*The Exorcist III* (1990), The Gemini Killer/James Venamun

*Mississippi Burning* (1988), Deputy Clinton Pell

*Child's Play* (1988), Charles Lee Ray/Voice of Chucky

*Blue Velvet* (1986), Raymond

*Dune* (1984), Piter De Vries

*Ragtime* (1981), Younger Brother

*Heaven's Gate* (1980), Mr. Eggleston

*Wise Blood* (1979), Hazel Motes

*Eyes of Laura Mars* (1978), Tommy Ludlow

*One Flew Over the Cuckoo's Nest* (1975), Billy Bibbit

# Joanne Dru

## 1922-1996

Born Joan Letitia La Cock in Logan, West Virginia, beautiful JOANNE DRU and her family moved to Wheeling when she was a child. She attended Wheeling High School before moving to New York following the death of her father.

The teenager soon found work as a John Powers model and a showgirl, dancing at the Paramount theatre where she met singer/actor Dick Haymes. In 1941, at the age of 19, Dru and Haymes were married. The newlyweds moved to California soon afterward, as Haymes had signed a film contract with 20th Century Fox. The couple eventually had two daughters and a son. As Haymes' film career began to ebb in the late 1940s, Joanne Dru's acting career started gaining momentum.

For her first film, she landed the starring role in *Abie's Irish Rose* (1946), but the film was not a success. Her next role, however, was in Howard Hawk's hit western *Red River* (1948; with John Wayne), in

# HOMETOWN
## West Virginia

WHEELING

which she co-starred with John Ireland. In 1949, Dru divorced Haymes and married Ireland. The couple made a number of films together, including *All the King's Men* (1949; with Broderick Crawford), *Vengeance Valley* (1951; with Burt Lancaster), *Hannah Lee* (1953; with Macdonald Carey) and *Southwest Passage* (1954; with Rod Cameron). Although she appeared in a healthy dose of dramas and film noir thrillers, due to her frequent appearances in westerns, Dru found herself typecast by the late 1950s.

Beyond 1960, Dru made just two more films. Throughout the 1960s, her acting career flourished on television, where she took guest spots in many shows, including *Guestward Ho!* and *Playhouse 90*. Dru's brother, comedian and game show host Peter Marshall, invited her to appear on *Hollywood Squares* numerous times in the 1960s and 1970s, but it never came to pass. After Dru's divorce from John Ireland in 1956, she married C. V. Wood, Jr., the industrialist who built Disneyland for Walt Disney. His passing in 1993 left her a widow. Three years later, on September 10, 1996, Joanne Dru passed away in Los Angeles.

OPPOSITE, TOP ] *Forbidden* with Tony Curtis; and *Red River* with John Wayne.

OPPOSITE, BOTTOM ] Dru with her brother Peter Marshall on her wedding day (1941).

# FILMOGRAPHY

*Super Fuzz* (1980) with Terence Hill and Ernest Borgnine
*Sylvia* (1965) with Carroll Baker, George Maharis, and Peter Lawford
*September Storm* (1960) with Mark Stevens
*The Wild and the Innocent* (1959) with Audie Murphy
*The Light in the Forest* (1958) with Fess Parker and Wendell Corey
*Drango* (1957) with Jeff Chandler and Julie London
*Hell on Frisco Bay* (1955) with Alan Ladd and Edward G. Robinson
*Sincerely Yours* (1955) with Liberace and Dorothy Malone
*The Dark Avenger* (1955) with Errol Flynn and Christopher Lee
*Day of Triumph* (1954) with Lee J. Cobb and Mike Connors
*Duffy of San Quentin* (1954) with Maureen O'Sullivan
*The Siege at Red River* (1954) with Van Johnson and Richard Boone
*Three Ring Circus* (1954) with Dean Martin, Jerry Lewis, and Zsa Zsa Gabor
*Southwest Passage* (1954) with John Ireland and Rod Cameron
*City of Bad Men* (1953) with Jeanne Crain, Dale Robertson, and Lloyd Bridges
*Forbidden* (1953) with Tony Curtis
*Hannah Lee* (1953) with John Ireland and Macdonald Carey
*Thunder Bay* (1953) with James Stewart and Gilbert Roland
*The Pride of St. Louis* (1952) with Dan Dailey
*My Pal Gus* (1952) with Richard Widmark
*Mr. Belvedere Rings the Bell* (1951) with Clifton Webb
*Vengeance Valley* (1951) with Burt Lancaster and John Ireland
*711 Ocean Drive* (1950) with Edmond O'Brien
*Wagon Master* (1950) with Ben Johnson
*All the King's Men* (1949) with Broderick Crawford
*She Wore a Yellow Ribbon* (1949) with John Wayne
*Red River* (1948) with John Wayne and John Ireland
*Abie's Irish Rose* (1946) with Micahel Chekhov

# Jennifer Garner

Courtesy of Charleston Magazine

JENNIFER GARNER, a Charleston, West Virginia, native, is a Golden Globe and Screen Actor's Guild winning actress for her performance in the ABC-TV program *Alias*. Garner has also been nominated two times for an Emmy, three times for a Golden Globe and two times for a Screen Actors Guild Award. *Alias* was awarded the People's Choice Award for Best New Drama Series. Garner portrays the lead character Sydney Bristow, a young woman who is a double agent attempting to live a normal life. *Alias* is in its fourth season and can be seen on Wednesday evenings at 9:00 PM (EST) on ABC. Garner recently signed on to Columbia Pictures' *Catch and Release*. She will begin filming in the summer of 2005.

Jennifer starred in the spin-off of Fox's *Daredevil* entitled *Elektra*. Prior to that performance, Garner was seen in Revolution Studios' smash hit *13 Going on 30*. Garner portrayed Jenna Rink, the 13 year-old who finds herself trapped in the body of a 30 year-old executive after a humiliating experience of 'Seven Minutes in the Closet.' Garner was also seen starring opposite Ben Affleck in Twentieth Century Fox's blockbuster hit *Daredevil*, based on the Marvel comic. The film also starred Colin Farrell, Michael Clarke Duncan and Jon Favreau.

Other film credits include *Pearl Harbor*, where she co-starred with Ben Affleck and Josh Hartnett in the World War II drama as the nurse Sandra alongside Kate Beckinsale and James King. Garner was also seen in the Twentieth Century Fox comedy *Dude, Where's My Car?* where she portrayed the female lead Wilma – the girlfriend of Ashton Kutcher.

Garner's additional feature film credits include *Mr. McGoo*, Woody Allen's *Deconstructing Harry, 1999* and *Washington Square*. Her television credits include a series regular role in both the Jennifer Love Hewitt drama *Time of Her Life* and the Bright/Kaufman/Krane drama *Significant Others*, as well as a recurring role on *Felicity*. She has guest starred on *Spin City, Law and Order* and has been featured in the television films *Rose Hill, Dead Man's Walk, Zoya* and *Harvest Fire*.

# HOMETOWN
### West Virginia

<small>CHARLESTON</small>

Photo: ABC Photo Archives

Garner has also participated in much off-screen work as a volunteer for many charitable organizations. She is an advocate for the Elizabeth Glaser Pediatric AIDS Foundation and is also involved with the National Breast Cancer Foundation. This past year, Jennifer volunteered her time to record a CIA Recruitment Video for our nation's Central Intelligence Agency.

Garner was born in Houston, raised in Charleston, West Virginia, and currently resides in Los Angeles with her dog Martha.

OPPOSITE, LEFT ] Featured on the cover of *Charleston Magazine* (2003).

ABOVE ] Garner with the cast of *Alias*.

# FROM THE SOUL

I grew up with parents who were committed to giving my sisters and me an education in the arts. We all took ballet and piano from a very early age. I have never had any ability in the visual arts, but I did grow up with a huge appreciation for beauty, thanks to living in the most beautiful place on the planet and having a mother obsessed with pointing out the natural wonders of West Virginia.

When I was nine I started studying ballet at Nina Denton Pasinetti's studio. She was an immediate and important influence on my life and my classes with her soon expanded into work with her company, The Appalachain Youth Jazz-Ballet Company. A couple of years later I followed Ms. Denton to her OTHER artistic outlet: The Charleston Light Opera Guild, the community theatre she runs as artistic director.

Ms. Denton taught an unruly bunch of girls about discipline, respect and the pride that comes with hard work. She also opened my eyes to possibilities with company trips to New York City. The community of Charleston is a much richer place for her numerous contributions.

When I describe myself I say first that I am the daughter of Bill and Pat Garner, second that I am the middle of three sisters and finally that I am a West Virginia girl. I love the community that raised me. I love the song that lifts from the mountains and trees and voices of the people that live there. I may not get home as often as I would like, but I carry my home state with me and try to make it proud.

# Lawrence Kasdan

LAWRENCE KASDAN has directed ten films: *Body Heat*, *The Big Chill*, *Silverado*, *The Accidental Tourist*, *I Love You To Death*, *Grand Canyon*, *Wyatt Earp*, *French Kiss*, *Mumford* and *Dreamcatcher*. He has written or co-written all of these pictures except John Kostmayer's *I Love You To Death* and Adam Brooks' *French Kiss*.

In addition, Kasdan has written or co-written four of the most successful films in motion picture history – *Raiders Of The Lost Ark*, *The Empire Strikes Back*, *Return Of The Jedi* and *The Bodyguard*.

Born in Miami Beach, Florida, and raised in West Virginia, Kasdan attended the University of Michigan, supporting himself with a series of writing awards while he studied English literature.

Kasdan made his critically acclaimed directorial debut with *Body Heat* in 1981. Next, he directed *The Big Chill*, which he co-wrote with Barbara Benedek and which was nominated for three Academy Awards, including Best Picture. His next effort was the sprawling western *Silverado*, which he directed and produced, and co-wrote with his brother Mark.

Kasdan next directed *The Accidental Tourist* based on the novel by Anne Tyler and adapted by Kasdan and Frank Galati. The film was named Best Picture of 1988 by the New York Film Critics, received four Academy Award nominations, including Best Picture, and earned Geena Davis a Best Supporting Actress award. 1990's *I Love You To Death*, written by John Kostmayer, was the first script that Kasdan directed that he did not write.

## HOMETOWN
### West Virginia

#### WHEELING

The script for *Grand Canyon*, co-written with his wife Meg Kasdan, earned them Academy Award and Golden Globe nominations for Best Original Screenplay. The film received the Golden Bear Award for Best Picture at the 1992 Berlin Film Festival.

In 1994, Kasdan made *Wyatt Earp*, starring Kevin Costner, Dennis Quaid and Gene Hackman, and in 1995, directed *French Kiss*, a romantic comedy set in Paris and Cannes with Meg Ryan and Kevin Kline.

Kasdan made his theatrical stage debut in the fall of 1995 as director of John Patrick Shanley's *Four Dogs and a Bone*, a dark comedic look at the seamier side of Hollywood, as the inaugural play of the newly renovated Geffen Playhouse.

*Mumford*, a comedy that Kasdan wrote and directed, and produced with Charles Okun, was released in 1999. At the San Sebastian Film Festival it won the award for Best Screenplay given by the Circle of Cinema Writers.

Kasdan most recently directed *Dreamcatcher*, based on the novel by Stephen King, for Castle Rock Entertainment and Warner Bros. Adapted for the screen by William Goldman and Lawrence Kasdan, the film was produced by Kasdan with Charles Okun. It was released in March, 2003.

OPPOSITE, TOP LEFT ] Kasdan with Steve Martin and Kevin Kline on the set of *Grand Canyon*.

OPPOSITE, TOP RIGHT ] Kasdan with Meg Ryan during the filming of *French Kiss*.

OPPOSITE, BOTTOM ] Kasdan with the men of *The Big Chill*.

THIS PAGE, TOP ] Kasdan on the set of *Silverado*.

THIS PAGE, BOTTOM ] Kasdan on the set of *Dreamcatcher*.

## FROM THE SOUL

I will always consider myself a West Virginian. My memory of my early years in Wheeling, my warm and welcoming neighborhood and local elementary school, are close to idyllic. Though my family had the usual amount of tumult, my own existence in the leafy beauty of our small town was very happy. And I think the experiences I had there – the freedom of the town granted by my bicycle, the constant companionship of my neighborhood friends – instilled in me some deep optimism that has sustained me even as I've experienced the outside world as an often difficult and challenging place.

In my career as a screenwriter and movie director, I have referred to my West Virginia youth in endless ways. That time has enriched my work and sent resounding ripples through the rest of my life. I think often and warmly of my beautiful home state.

# Don Knotts

TAGSRWC Archives

Few actors successfully bridge the gap between television and motion pictures. DON KNOTTS is one of the select few who have made it.

The star of 19 motion pictures, his own hour television variety series and several specials, Don is no stranger to comedy. He has won five coveted Emmy Awards for his flawless portrayal as Barney Fife on *The Andy Griffith Show*, appeared on Broadway (and in the film version) in *No Time for Sergeants* and established himself as one of our top comedic actors in all these media.

Don was born in Morgantown, West Virginia. To be in show business was his ambition from boyhood and, aside from getting an education, it's about all he's ever known. As a child he was a movie aficionado and constant radio fan, concentrating on comedy shows. His idol was Jack Benny and, even at the age of twelve, Don was aware of, and tried to copy, Benny's impeccable timing.

Another of his favorite radio shows was Edgar Bergen's, which inspired him to learn ventriloquism. Throughout high school he entertained civic groups with an act which he admits was "borrowed" from Mr. Bergen.

After graduating from high school, Don enrolled as a speech major at West Virginia University, fully intending to become a teacher. However, the Army called, and instead he spent the next couple of years touring the South Pacific, doing comedy routines in *Stars and Gripes*. It was only natural that the thus bitten Don would finish his college education and head for New York City and show business.

The next few years saw Don appearing on various radio and television programs until he landed a role in *No Time for Sergeants*. During the run of the Broadway hit, Don began creating comedy material – thus was born the "nervous little man," a character so familiar to audiences and based on an after dinner speaker he once observed back home in Morgantown.

Next came the Gary Moore and Steve Allen shows. In 1959 Don elected to move to Hollywood when the *Steve Allen Show* did, later joining Andy Griffith in the legendary series that made him and his Deputy Barney Fife character a household name. Don's portrayal of the Mayberry deputy won him five Emmys.

# HOMETOWN
### West Virginia
## MORGANTOWN

The rigors of weekly television convinced Don that making motion pictures had to be less arduous, but he was finally lured back into the fold as Ralph Furley, a regular on the hit weekly show *Three's Company*. Don also made a few rare guest appearances on other television shows, including *Matlock*, reuniting him once again with Andy Griffith.

Having performed in all phases of the entertainment industry, Don enjoys appearing in legitimate theater, and a typical year will encompass his three big loves – motion pictures, television and theater. He claims he enjoys the best of all entertainment worlds without limiting himself to any one facet.

Don makes his home in Los Angeles.

OPPOSITE, LEFT ] Don with Jim Nabors on *The Andy Griffith Show*.

ABOVE, RIGHT ] Don with Betty "Thelma Lou" Lynn and Andy Griffith at his Hollywood Walk of Fame ceremony (2000); Don with one of his five Emmys.

## FILMOGRAPHY

*No Time for Sergeants*
*It's a Mad Mad Mad Mad World*
*Move Over Darling*
*The Incredible Mr. Limpet*
*The Ghost and Mr. Chicken*
*The Reluctant Astronaut*
*The Shakiest Gun in the West*
*The Love God?*
*How to Frame a Fig*
*Apple Dumpling Gang*
*Gus*
*No Deposit, No Return*
*Herbie Goes to Monte Carlo*
*Hot Lead, Cold Feet*
*Apple Dumpling Gang Rides Again*
*The Prize Fighter*
*The Private Eyes*
*Cannonball Run II*
*Pleasantville*

# FROM THE SOUL

My ambition to become an actor goes as far back as I can remember. I was so committed, in fact, that the possibility of becoming something else never even occurred to me. I suppose it all started with my mother. She was a devoted movie fan, and she started taking me to the movies along about the time talking pictures were coming in. I must've been about five years old. Laurel and Hardy and Abbott and Costello soon became my favorite funny men. Like so many of my peers, my idol on the radio was Jack Benny. It was a dream come true, some thirty years later, when I shared the stage with Mr. Benny on a television special on CBS.

My four high school years were the happiest and most fertile of my life (not counting *The Andy Griffith Show*). Whatever inhibitions and uncertainties I may have felt in my early youth, they melted away the day I walked through the front door of Morgantown High School. I began to experience a great sense of fun and an immense release of creative energy. I wrote a humorous column for the school newspaper, wrote sketches for shows, MC'd assembly programs and appeared in high school plays. In short, I had a ball. I also formed a lot of new friendships, some I cherish to this day.

*Don Knotts*

# Ann Magnuson

ANN MAGNUSON is an actress, singer, writer and performance artist whose chameleon-like persona has found expression in everything from TV sitcoms and Hollywood blockbusters to art galleries and underground rock clubs.

Audiences who know her as the lovesick FBI secretary who gets her neck snapped in the Harrison Ford thriller *Clear and Present Danger* may not realize she was also singer and lyricist for the infamous psycho-psychedelic cult band Bongwater. Those who enjoyed her as the eccentric magazine editor in the ABC-TV sitcom *Anything But Love* probably don't know she was also the disco-punk chick David Bowie makes deadly vampire love to in the chic horror film *The Hunger*.

Some may have seen her star in the 1987 film *Making Mr. Right* in which she plays the object of John Malkovich's robot-affection. Others may only know her as a magazine writer who has interviewed everyone from Cher to the Red Hot Chili Peppers.

Born and raised in Charleston, West Virginia, Magnuson graduated from Denison University in 1978 with a degree in Theater & Cinema. After spending her junior year abroad (studying theater in London), she spent her final semester interning at New York's Ensemble Studio Theater. She then moved to the East Village where she co-founded and managed the now-legendary, neo-Dada Club 57. She ran the club from 1978 until 1981 and was a prominent figure in downtown Manhattan's art and music scene.

During the '80s and early '90s, Ann developed and performed in hundreds of theater, nightclub and performance art venues, creating a gallery of serio-comic characters, many of which were showcased in *Made For TV*, the 1984 video that premiered on the PBS series *Alive From Off Center*.

# HOMETOWN
## West. Virginia

### CHARLESTON

Ann has been seen off-Broadway in *The Vagina Monologues, Four Dogs and a Bone* and in her own one-woman show *You Could Be Home Now*, which originated at the Serious Fun Festival at Lincoln Center in 1987. The show was re-conceived at The New York Shakespeare Festival's Joseph Papp Public Theater where it enjoyed a sold out run in 1992. It later enjoyed a successful tour throughout 1993.

Alternating between dramatic and comedic roles, Ann has appeared in over thirty films including *Panic Room, The Caveman's Valentine, A Night in the Life of Jimmy Reardon* and *Desperately Seeking Susan*, as well as countless indie-films including *Night at the Golden Eagle* and *The United States of Leland*. Television appearances include *From the Earth to the Moon, The Drew Carey Show, Frasier* and her own Cinemax comedy special, *Vandemonium*. Ann's solo album, *The Luv Show,* was released by Geffen Records in 1995, and in 2001, *Rave Mom* – an ecstasy-laced monologue about the 'irrational exuberance' of 1999 (see photo with alien) – premiered in New York City.

Ann continues to write and perform her unique "alternative cabaret" musicals. She lives with her husband, architect John Bertram, in Los Angeles, where she is also performing *Pretty Songs & Ugly Stories* (a mix of music and spoken word) that will be released on CD in 2005.

OPPOSITE, TOP] (l-r) Magnuson with the cast of *Anything But Love* (1990); Magunson with John Malcovich in *Making Mr. Right* (1987).

ABOVE ] Performing her *Tribute to Muzak* in the elevator of NYC's Whitney Museum.

# FROM THE SOUL

I remember finger painting as the greatest thrill in the world. At Holz Elementary, I also recall a radio program called Talking Pictures that catered to the entire state school system. Classes would stop at an appointed time and we would listen to a piece of music and then create a piece of artwork that reflected the mood or story of the piece. My mother narrated Stravinsky's *The Firebird* one week, which may have confused my second grade brain, but, like my television debut on the local *Romper Room* show, it also instilled in me the idea that there were no real obstacles to getting on TV or radio.

The public school system provided me with my first acting role (as the littlest Billy Goat in *The Billy Goats Gruff* performed at my second grade graduation ceremony) and exposed me to classic folk tunes like *A Froggy Went A-Courtin'* in our daily music hour. In fourth grade, one of my favorite teachers had a thing for Peter, Paul and Mary, so I inadvertently got an education in social protest, as well as three-part harmony.

I took ballet in Charleston from Mr. Van Damme and later took tap and modern dance from Nina Lu Denton, who was also my algebra teacher at George Washington High School. I also performed in shows and took journalism classes at G.W. that eventually led to my becoming the editorial writer, then short-term editor, of the school newspaper.

Still, it was growing up in the lush green hills of Almost Heaven that has been the greatest gift of them all, created by that ultimate artist whom the rest of us simply try to imitate.

*Ann Magnuson*

# Peter Marshall

Born Pierre La Cock in Huntington, West Virginia, PETER MARSHALL made his entrance into show business as a band singer at the age of 15. While still a teen, he moved to New York City where he landed a job as a page in radio for NBC.

Early in his career he joined forces with Tommy Noonan. The comedy team appeared in major night clubs, films and theatres throughout the country and made numerous appearances on *The Ed Sullivan Show*.

Peter soon went to London and starred with Chita Rivera in *Bye Bye Birdie*. His first starring role on Broadway was with Julie Harris in *Skyscraper*. In later years, he appeared in other musicals including *High Button Shoes, Anything Goes, Music Man, 42nd Street* and Neil Simon's *Rumors*.

Of course, Peter is best-known for hosting over 5,000 episodes of *Hollywood Squares*, for which he won five "Best Game Show Host" Emmy Awards. After appearing in a commercial for Kelloggs, Peter was asked to audition for the show, and the rest is television history. With guests including Paul Lynde, Rose Marie, Charlie Weaver, George Gobel, Wally Cox and some of the greatest entertainers in history, Hollywood Squares entertained audiences for over 15 years!

Peter has guest-starred on many major television series such as *The Love Boat, Lou Grant, WKRP in Cincinnati* and *Sabrina the Teenage Witch*. He's also appeared in several mini-series'. He is proud of his performance in *HMS Pinafore* with the London Symphony Orchestra, which has been seen on the big screen as well as on television.

With such a profound musical background and a great love of music, Peter thoroughly enjoyed hosting a series of 12 shows for the Disney Channel, *Big Bands from Disneyland*, with such celebrated bands and leaders as Woody Herman, Lionel Hampton and Buddy Rich. He has produced and toured in big band shows featuring Tex Beneke and his Orchestra, the Modernaires with Paula Kelly, Jr., and singers such as Helen O'Connell, Helen Forrest and Frankie Laine.

Currently, Peter is heard nationally on the *Music Of Your Life* radio network. His popular daily show features the music of the Big Band era and offers his vast insight into this wonderful era of great music.

# HOMETOWN
### West Virginia

### HUNTINGTON

In 2000, Peter's CD *Boy Singer* was released with critical acclaim. The CD, which was recorded at Capitol Records, features beautiful standards with new arrangements by some of the most renowned arrangers of big band music, and a full 36-piece orchestra.

Peter Marshall's career has demonstrated a versatility and flexibility that few entertainers can match. He's successfully conquered nearly every genre of entertainment including stage and screen, movies and television, radio, records and CDs and, with his www.boysinger.com website, the internet.

Even with such a remarkable career, Peter's easy-going and humble personality remains, which undoubtedly contributes to his being one of the most well-liked personalities in the entertainment industry.

OPPOSITE, LEFT ] Cover of *Backstage with the Original Hollywood Square* by Marshall and Adrienne Armstrong.

ABOVE ] *No Happy Endings: A Tribute to the Lady in Satin* featuring Marshall and the music of Ray Ellis (2003).

TOP, RIGHT] Marshall with Ray Ellis.

## FROM THE SOUL

I remember my first teacher, Mrs. Gable. She used to tell me how handsome I was, and I was so honored by that. It's amazing how certain words from teachers or other people in your life stay with you.

My father died when I was ten. We moved to Huntington where I attended school with Soupy Sales. I went to New York when I was 12 and attended high schools there and in Connecticut. When I was almost 17, I returned to Huntington. The war was on, and if I didn't get a diploma, I would have been inducted into the infantry. The principal, Mr. Brewer, was a wonderful man. I had two years of high school yet to finish, but he arranged my schedule so that I could get my diploma in one year…and that's what happened. I subsequently served in the Artillery in World War II from 1944 to 1946.

While I was in high school, an English teacher, Mrs. MacMillan, who had been a friend of my mother and father's growing up, felt I wasn't living up to my abilities. She told me that I wouldn't go very far in life and wouldn't amount to anything at the rate I was going. I never forgot her words.

In 1961, I was in London at Her Majesty's Theatre appearing with Chita Rivera in *Bye Bye Birdie*. My valet came backstage and told me that there was a Mrs. MacMillan who wanted to come say hello to me. It was wonderful to see her. She told me that she had retired and was now traveling the globe, visiting the places she had taught about for so many years. Whether teachers are positive or negative, the most important thing is to believe in yourself.

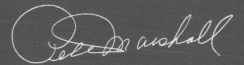

# Beth McVey

BETH MCVEY continues to work steadily as a professional actress, adding to her already impressive body of work. She has worked on Broadway with legendary directors such as Gower Champion in the original cast of *42nd Street* and Tommy Tune in his Tony Award-winning production of *Nine*, performing the roles of Claudia, Carla and Francesca. She has also played featured roles in the long-running Broadway hits *Annie*, as Star to Be and Lily St. Regis, *Phantom of the Opera*, as Carlotta and Madame Firman and *Beauty and the Beast* as the maternal Mrs. Potts.

Beth's other New York credits include her opera debut in *The Merry Widow* at New York City Opera and City Center Encores! productions of *Call Me Madame, Dubarry Was A Lady, On A Clear Day, A Tree Grows in Brooklyn* and *The Coffee Club Orchestra 10th Anniversary*. She has also been seen as Mrs. Claus in *The Radio City Christmas Spectacular*.

Her touring credits include Ms. Pennywise in *Urinetown*, Adelaide in *Guys and Dolls*, Gladys in *Copacabana* and Dianna in *Lend Me A Tenor*. Beth has worked extensively in regional theatres across the country, playing leads in shows such as

# HOMETOWN
## West Virginia

### HUNTINGTON

# FROM THE SOUL

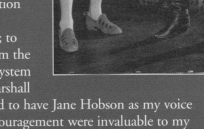

From my earliest memories all I ever wanted to do was perform. Thankfully my teachers recognized that desire and gave me as many opportunities as they were able. From singing *Frosty the Snowman* in the 2nd grade Christmas program to singing at my high school graduation, teachers like Caroline Stone at Lincoln Junior High and Betty O'Shel, Robert Vie and Catherine Cummings at Huntington High gave their students not only an appreciation for the arts, but also the encouragement to participate; to spread our wings and fly. From the West Virginia public school system I continued my studies at Marshall University where I was blessed to have Jane Hobson as my voice teacher. Her training and encouragement were invaluable to my success as a performer.

It's so important to give children the opportunity to express themselves, to encourage them to use their imaginations and to teach them an appreciation for the arts. To quote graphic artist and computer scientist John Maeda, "The Arts are the Science of enjoying Life." I certainly have enjoyed my career and I look forward to passing on that knowledge and love.

*Beth McVey*

*Thoroughly Modern Millie; Nine; Mame; Man of La Mancha; Pirates of Penzance; A Little Night Music; The Sound of Music; Showboat; Oliver; Anything Goes; Kiss Me, Kate; Evita;* and many others.

Beth's other performing credits include many workshops, daytime dramas and televised concerts. She has also been seen performing her nightclub act throughout the country.

A graduate of the Cincinnati Conservatory of Music, Beth – who is also Miss West Virginia 1973 – recently moved back to her home town of Huntington where she is a

board member for ARTS (Art Resources for the Tri-State) and is directing, coaching and teaching a new generation of musical artists.

OPPOSITE, TOP ] McVey as Reno in the musical *Anything Goes.*

ABOVE ] McVey as Penelope Pennywise in *Urinetown: The Musical.*

ABOVE, RIGHT ] McVey in *Man of La Mancha.*

## J. Mark McVey

J. MARK McVEY is proud to be a part of this publication. Mr. McVey made his PBS debut in 2003 with the Boston Pops, and followed that performance with a PBS Christmas Special for U.S. troops, where he was featured with Marvin Hamlisch and The National Symphony Orchestra.

J. Mark McVey made his Carnegie Hall debut in 1997 with Mr. Hamlisch and is Marvin's tenor of choice for symphony concerts. J. Mark has performed with numerous symphonies across the world, including Boston, Chicago, Detroit, Philadelphia, New York, Baltimore, Pittsburgh, The National Symphony, Dallas, Houston, Toronto, Montreal, Calgary, Vancouver, Jerusalem and numerous others.

Best known for his theatre work, McVey made his Broadway debut as Jean Valjean in *Les Misérables* after having won the Helen Hayes Award for Outstanding Actor while in the show's Washington, D.C., production. He was also the first American to perform that role in London's West End. In February, 2003, he completed his seventh full year as Jean Valjean with over 2,900 performances.

Other Broadway credits and New York successes include: Captain Walker in *The Who's Tommy;* Tommy Tune's *The Best Little Whorehouse Goes Public;* the off-Broadway revival of *Chess; Hey Love,* the critically acclaimed review of Mary Rodgers music, conceived and directed by Richard Maltby, Jr.; *A Helluva Town,*

## HOMETOWN
### West Virginia

HUNTINGTON

*"With his shock of blonde hair and powerful tenor, Mr. McVey belongs to the dwindling ranks of dashing leading men."*

–*New York Times*

the Bernstein review at Rainbow & Stars where Mark enjoyed rave reviews; and *The Show Goes On*, with Tom Jones and Harvey Schmidt, where he can be heard on his first cast album. National tours and regional works include *Carousel, My Fair Lady, South Pacific, Seven Brides* and *Showboat*, directed by Hal Prince.

Mark's solo CDs – *Broadway and Beyond, If You Really Knew Me: The Music of Marvin Hamlisch* and *One Among Few* – can be purchased on the internet at www.jmarkmcvey.com or www.marimackproductions.com.

Mark is married to Christy Tarr and is the proud father of two beautiful daughters, four year old Grace Holly and eighteen month old Kylie Elizabeth. Beth McVey, also a successful performer, is J. Mark's sister.

J. Mark McVey hails from Huntington, West Virginia, and thanks God for his gifts, his family and friends for their tireless support, and he would like to thank you for supporting the Arts.

OPPOSITE, TOP ] The cast of *Les Misérables;* Mark as Jean Valjean.

# FROM THE SOUL

In these times, when public schools nationwide are being forced to cut budgets, inevitably the first programs to fall by the wayside are music and art. This brings me sorrow and disappointment for the young minds that are being deprived of the opportunity to develop a well-rounded education and, thus, a brighter outlook for the future of our great nation. It is a well-documented fact that students who are able to benefit from art and music score higher on their college entrance exams than students not given that chance.

When I recall my own personal experiences, it is with great joy that I express my gratitude for the opportunities the West Virginia public school system afforded me in my formidable years. Had it not been for the music and art programs – the outlet for my emotional and psychological development – I would have been in a lot of trouble.

All my teachers deserve credit for aiding in my development. *Thanks!* And several teachers deserve mention for their uncommon abilities in helping develop my special gifts: Mrs. Toothman at Meadows Elementary, Mrs. Stone and Mrs. White at Lincoln Junior High School and Mr. Buel at Huntington High School.

I believe these teachers had the wonderful gift to identify, develop and direct a student's talents, making them more aware of their own unique abilities and, thus, more comfortable and confident. With self-confidence an individual is more aware and better able to identify and appreciate the abilities of those around them.  By developing students in this manner, these teachers not only made each individual student more interested in the class they were taking, but also better equipped to face the world in which we live. And for that I say *thank you* from the bottom of my heart!

*J. Mark McVey*

# Lou Myers

LOU MYERS can be seen in *The Fighting Temptations, Friday After Next, The Wedding Planner, Lakawana Blues* (Showtime) and has been seen in such movies as *Passions of Darkly Noon* (Showtime*), How Stella Got Her Groove Back, Bullworth, Tin Cup, Cobb, Volcano, Everything's Jake, The Stand In, All About You* and *Goodbye Lover.* He is best know as the irascible restaurant owner, Mr. Gaines, on the hit television series *A Different World.* Lou wrote, produced and co-directed his critically acclaimed one-man show *Just A Little Bit Of Somethin'* off-Broadway in New York City.

Lou has come a long way from the mountains of West Virginia. Struggling all alone he managed to finish college and attend graduate school at New York University before appearing on Broadway in *The Piano Lesson,* Ma Rainey's *Black Bottom* and *The First Breeze of Summer.* Lou recently won the NAACP Best Actor Award for his work on August Wilson's *King Hedley II* in the role of Sole Pigeon. He previously won the off-Broadway Delco Award for his role in *Fat Tuesday.* He was founder and director of the Tshaka Ensemble Players, which toured in the acclaimed play, *Shakespeare's Julius Caesar,* set in Africa. He served as the griot and dancer for several dance companies, such as the Dinizula Dancers and Drummers and Singers. He has narrated their stories in three languages – French, German and Spanish.

He began singing Jazz and Blues with the touring company of Negro Music in *Vogue.* His cabaret show has been acclaimed in Berlin, Paris, Hong Kong, Tokyo and New York, as well as Los Angeles at the Roosevelt Hotel.

His other television credits include: *NYPD Blue, EVE, All About the Andersons, E.R., Malcolm & Eddie, Jet Jackson, The Cosby Show, Touched By An Angel, JAG, The Sentinel, Bag Dad Café, The Sinbad Show, Living Single, Thea, The Jamie Foxx Show, Mama Flores Family, Private Affair* and *Riot.*

Lou still gets inspiration from his mother, Dorothy Myers-Jeffries, and his son, Melvin Myers, who is presently attending graduate school. Lou is a board member, Chief Enlightenment Officer and Corporate Storyteller for Global Business Incubation, Inc. (GBI) 501 (c)(3), a research development organization that catalyzes the business

# HOMETOWN
## West Virginia

### CHESAPEAKE

# FROM THE SOUL

West Virginia schools have served me well, and I have many fond memories. My first day of school was anticipated with great excitement. My father, Otis Myers, had taught me my ABCs and I knew them well. My mother, Dorothy, walked me to the bus stop where we waited with the other mothers and children for the big yellow bus to come.

Ms. Bimas, one of my favorite teachers, told stories about the Indians and the Dutch. We painted pictures and built paper mache wigwams and windmills. This was my first contact with my imagination...with traveling outside of West Virginia.

Miss Alfreda Turner taught 7th grade English and drama. I was in one of her plays and remember on the night of the show, Henry Camaron, who had a role in the play, was in an accident and couldn't get to the school. I had to play a double role – my first time working under pressure.

In high school, Mr. Brown taught history and was also director of the band, where I learned to play the trombone. The West Virginia school system made me feel good, like I was a part of the community.

I left school in the 11th grade and joined the Air Force, where I earned my G.E.D. I returned home to attend West Virginia State College and graduated with a B.A. in Psychology and Sociology. I went on to study at New York University. I have based my career in movies, television and theater on the education I received in West Virginia schools.

*Lou Myers*

development process of launching an idea, a business and a community through growing cooperative business incubator cluster models that grow companies. Mr. Myers is also Chairman of the Urban Futurist Organization and The Lou Myers Scenario Motion Picture Institute.

OPPOSITE, LEFT ] Myers with the cast of *A Different World*.

ABOVE ] (l-r) Myers as Sole Pigeon in August Wilson's *King Hedley II*; U.S. Air Force portrait.

# Soupy Sales

SOUPY SALES, one of the most beloved and renowned comedians ever, received his star on the famous Hollywood Walk of Fame on January 7, 2005. At the event, the Mayor of Hollywood insisted on getting a pie in his face; Soupy was delighted to comply. Yes, the Soup is still hot!

Born in North Carolina, Soupy grew up in Huntington, West Virginia, where he first became interested in dramatics while in high school. Later, while a student at Marshall University, he eyed a career in journalism and received a B.A. in this chosen field. He landed a job as a radio scriptwriter for a small station in Huntington. His high energy and glib gift-for-gab led to a disc jockey spot and, after becoming the top-rated DJ at WHTN in Huntington, he left for Cincinnati where he starred in his first television show. The year was 1950, and *Soupy's Soda Shop* became American television's first teenage dance program.

From Cincinnati, Soupy went on to perform in Cleveland before moving to Detroit in 1953, where he started his fantastic television rise and became the Motor City's top-rated TV personality for nearly a decade. (Years later, Soupy received an Emmy from the Detroit Chapter of the National Television Academy.) His Friday night show will long be remembered by the American TV-viewing public for its classic climax, where the surprise guests, along with Soupy, received a custard-cream pie smack in the face. Frank Sinatra, a huge fan of the show, actually called to book himself as a guest. Soupy has received over 19,000 pies since he has been on TV.

In September 1964, Soupy brought *The Soupy Sales Show* to New York where it soon became the biggest show of its kind in local television. In 1966, the show went national and was seen throughout the U.S., as well as in Canada, Australia and New Zealand.

Aside from having his own network show, Soupy would make guest appearances on other shows such as *The Tonight Show, The Carol Burnett Show* and *The Bob Hope Show.* When Soupy appeared on *The Ed Sullivan Show,* Sullivan broke an 18-year precedent by inviting Soupy back for the following Sunday – something unheard of and never before done.

In 1966 Soupy left his TV show to venture into the New York theater scene. His debut play *Come Live With Me* received mixed reviews. Not one to be discouraged by the critics, Soupy wrote and starred in another

FROM THE SOUL

play, the 1967 World's Fair Expo hit *Hellzapoppin*. In 1968, he returned to TV, joining the panel of the hit show *What's My Line*, where as a regular panelist appeared in 1,500 shows.

Through the early '70s, Soupy started breaking in his nightclub act as he continued his television work. As the '80s arrived, so did more Soupy Sales fans after seeing him in clubs, on game shows and as a semi-regular on *TV's Bloopers and Practical Jokes*.

A long-time resident of New York, home to the beloved comedian is Manhattan's east side. Not the only one in his family to have made a career in show business, Soupy's sons, Hunt and Tony, are accomplished musicians who have played with some of the greatest rock bands. Soupy is married to former Rockette, Trudy Carson.

Soupy Sales received one of the biggest distinctions of his colorful life and career when his alma mater, Marshall University, in Huntington, West Virginia, bestowed him an honorary Doctorate of Humane Letters degree. In his announcement

of the honor, former University president Dale F. Nitzschke said, "Soupy Sales is unquestionably one of this country's comic geniuses. He has brought distinction to himself and honor to his hometown and university."

Soupy responded, "I'll make house calls."

OPPOSITE, LEFT ] *The Soupy Sales Show.*

About a year after my father died, when I was six years old, I made my stage debut playing Peter Rabbit. It was without a doubt the pivotal event of my life because when I heard those two hundred or so people laughing and clapping, I felt like a bolt of lightening had struck me. To this day, I think the thing that makes me the happiest is the applause and laughter I get from an audience…and the unhappiest is the reality that you can't work all the time, which means that the applause and laughter is limited to the time you're actually performing. I know all you amateur head shrinkers out there are probably nodding your heads and saying, "Well that's why he's in show business…he needs constant reassurance, constant demonstrations of love." And the truth is, you may be right. I am a workaholic, but I also love to entertain people. I love to make them smile. And even if I'd listened to my parents and become an optician, I suspect I'd be a very funny one.

Anyway, I don't know whether it was a message from God or not, but after that gig as Peter Rabbit I said to myself, "Soupy, this is what you're going to do with the rest of your life." It's weird, I know, because I was only six years old. Yet somehow I knew that entertaining people was going to be my life.

# Chris Sarandon

CHRIS SARANDON was born and raised in Beckley, West Virginia. His Greek immigrant father ran a restaurant there. His mother was the daughter of immigrant Greeks. After high school, he attended West Virginia University where he received his B.A. magna cum laude.

After receiving his M.F.A. in Theatre at the Catholic University of America in Washington, D.C., he joined the Long Wharf Theatre Company for a season. He then moved to New York where, after a short stint on the soap opera *The Guiding Light*, he was cast as Jacob Rothschild in the original Broadway production of *The Rothschilds*. He also replaced Raul Julia in the New York Shakespeare Festival's hit Broadway musical *The Two Gentlemen of Verona*.

He also has appeared at the New York Shakespeare Festival in the New York premiere of *The Woods* by David Mamet and in the world premiere of John Guare's *Marco Polo Sings a Solo* with Sigorney Weaver, Joel Grey and Madeline Kahn. He co-starred with Rex Harrison in Shaw's *The Devil's Disciple* with the BAM Theatre Company, played Marchbanks in Shaw's *Candida* at Canada's acclaimed Shaw Festival and co-starred in the Broadway musical *Nick and Nora*.

Sarandon made his film debut as Al Pacino's confused lover in *Dog Day Afternoon*, for which he was nominated for an Academy Award as Best Supporting Actor. His other screen appearances include roles in *Cuba* with Sean

## HOMETOWN
### West Virginia

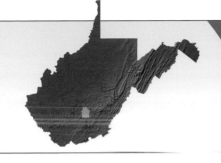

*"The rich artistic landscape...the spectacular visual setting of my hometown...became the template for my thirst to continue as a performing artist."*

Connery; Sam Peckinpah's last film, *The Osterman Weekend*; the Herbert Ross directed *Protocol*, starring Goldie Hawn; and Rob Reiner's *The Princess Bride* as the evil Prince Humperdink. He also starred as the suave, sophisticated vampire in the cult classic *Fright Night* and as the anguished policeman chasing the demented doll Chucky in the original *Child's Play*.

His TV appearances include starring roles in Hallmark Hall of Fame's *A Tale of Two Cities* and *You Can't Go Home Again*, as well as guest appearances on *Picket Fences*, *The Practice*, *Law and Order* and recurring roles on *Felicity*, *E.R.* and *Judging Amy*. He also recently co-starred in producer John Well's Supreme Court drama *The Court*, starring Sally Field.

Sarandon was tapped by creator Tim Burton to be the speaking voice of the lead character Jack Skellington in the stop-action animation classic *The Nightmare Before Christmas*, and he will be soon heard in the new animated features, *The Chosen One* and Hayao Miyazaki's *Nausica*.

Sarandon developed, produced and stared in *Road Ends*, a feature film also starring Dennis Hopper, Peter Coyote and Mariel Hemingway. He also wrote, produced and directed the short film *Snowfall*. He is married to actress/writer/director Joanna Gleason and they have four children: Aaron Gleason and Stephanie, Alexis and Michael Sarandon.

OPPOSITE, TOP ] Sarandon with writer/director Tom Holland on the set of *Fright Night* (1985).

## FROM THE SOUL

It's 1958. Picture a 15 year-old boy with "pegged" pants and a "DA" hair-do, shirt collar turned up...yep, "Grease" all the way. But this boy was not just interested in cars and girls and combing that hair: he had a yen to perform. He was musical (church choir, listening to jazz and R & B) and bought a used set of drums.

At that time the musical scene in Beckley, West Virginia, was mostly country and bluegrass. But Rock and Roll was just being born: juke boxes began to hum with the music of Little Richard, Chuck Berry, the Everly Brothers and Elvis, defining a new kind of musical expression. And the boy, with some kids from Beckley's Woodrow Wilson High School band (they were real musicians), formed a Rock and Roll band, The Teen Tones. The boys became a pretty fine band, even wrote and recorded some songs and toured, playing with or backing up such top nationally known recording artists as Bobby Darin and Carl Perkins.

That boy, of course, was (is) me. The rich artistic/musical landscape of school mates and teachers, coupled with the spectacular visual setting of my hometown, all became the template for my thirst to continue as a performing artist. Without that combination, I'd have become what my father wanted me to be: Famous Brain Surgeon Dr. Chris Sarandon; Supreme Court Justice Chris Sarandon. But then as an actor, I got to be both...and have many other fantasy lives as well. What a lucky fellow that boy turned out to be!

# David Selby

DAVID SELBY was born and raised in Morgantown, West Virginia. He received both his B.A. and M.A. from West Virginia University and a Ph.D. from Southern Illinois University. He is an honorary member of the WVU Creative Arts Center's Advisory Board, has worked with the Governor's Honor Academy and has made many appearances around the state of West Virginia.

In 1989 he was honored as a Distinguished Alumnus of WVU and, in May of 1992, received the Distinguished Alumnus Award from the College of Communications and Fine Art at SIU. He was inducted into the Cleveland Playhouse Hall of Fame in 1994 and in 1998 was given the first Life Achievement Award by the WVU College of Creative Arts. In 1999, Selby received the Millennium Recognition Award from the Shakespeare Theatre in Washington, D.C., and in 2002 was presented the Distinguished West Virginian Award. In 2004, Selby was awarded an honorary doctorate from WVU.

David Selby began his professional career in regional theatres such as the Barter Theatre and the Cleveland Playhouse. He has starred in *The Children's Hour* with Joanne Woodward and Shirley Knight, *The Devil's Disciple* with Jill Clayburgh and *The Heiress* with Jane Alexander and Richard Kiley.

His long list of Broadway and off-Broadway plays also includes David Rabe's *Sticks and Bones*, N. Richard Nash's *Echoes* and Sam Shephard's *Forensic and the Navigator*. In Los Angeles, Selby received Drama Logue Awards for his portrayals of both John Proctor in *The Crucible* and the Rev. T. Lawrence Shannon in *Night of the Iguana*.

Selby's feature films include *Rich and Famous* with Candice Bergin and Jackie Bissett; *Rich Kids* with John Lithgow; *Up the Sandbox* with Barbra Streisand; *Dying Young* with Julia Roberts; *Alone* with Hume Cronyn and James Earl Jones; *Surviving Christmas* with Ben Affleck and James Gandolfini; and *Shadow of Fear* with James Spader, Peter Coyote and Aidan Quinn.

For television, Selby created the roles of Quentin Collins on *Dark Shadows*, Michael Tyrone on *Flamingo Road* and Richard Channing on *Falcon Crest*. Television credits also include numerous movies of the week and guest starring roles on several series,

# HOMETOWN
## West Virginia
### MORGANTOWN

including *Mind of the Married Man* and David E. Kelley's hit FOX-TV show *Ally McBeal*.

He enjoys his involvement recording classics before live audiences for L.A. Theatre Works' National Public Radio series. Among numerous appearances, he recreated his stage role in Joyce Carol Oates' *The Perfectionist* and starred in Lillian Hellman's *The Autumn Garden* with Julie Harris, Eric Stolz and Mary Steenburgen. For the

BBC, he has recorded *On the Waterfront* and *A Streetcar Named Desire*.

Also an accomplished writer, Selby has penned the plays *Lincoln and James*, *The Final Assault* and *Where's Nova Scotia?*. His books include *In and Out of the Shadows*, a poetry collection titled *My Mother's Autumn* and *Happenstance*, a second book of poetry. His production company currently has a number of projects in development. Selby and his wife, Chip, a native of Beckley, West Virginia, have three children. They make their home in Los Angeles.

OPPOSITE, LEFT ] Selby delivering WVU's 135th Commencement Speech.

TOP, LEFT ] Selby receiving his Honorary Doctorate from WVU President David Hardesty (2004).

## FROM THE SOUL

An excerpt from David's original poem

### *West Virginia*

Surrounded
  but still the lost island.
  I write your name
   idle fingers through my hair
   years and miles away
   cooling shadows across
   your moonlit walls
   "how majestic and how grand"
   still a part of me
   you reached the marrow
   touched the contours of my soul.
   Cradled in your walls
   my likeness, even now, flavored
   by your lilting tongue
   my short leg from walking your walls
   my white face from living in your hollows
  my boundaries you drew
  teaching step by step
 to climb your narrow walls
  to ride the crest
 of your highest wave
 down to other shores
 a branded calf
a hill child.

*David Selby*

WV Dept. of Tourism

# Morgan Spurlock

Photo: Julie Soefer

MORGAN SPURLOCK is an award-winning writer, producer and director. Originally from Beckley, West Virginia, he graduated from New York University's Tisch School of the Arts in 1993.

His first feature length play, *The Phoenix*, won the Audience Award at the 1998 New York International Fringe Festival. Spurlock went on to win the Outstanding Playwright prize at the Route 66 National Playwright Competition in 1999.

Spurlock's first TV series, *I Bet You Will*, premiered on MTV in March, 2002, and was the first show ever to make the jump from the internet to television. After producing 53 episodes of the reality game show, he took his profits and poured them into his first feature film, the fast food exposé *Super Size Me*.

In 2004, *Super Size Me* became the third highest grossing documentary of all time. Spurlock won the Best Director prizes at the Sundance and Edinburgh Film Festivals. The movie was named to more than 35 year-end top ten lists and was a National Board of Review and Critic's Choice Best Documentary nominee. New York Film Critics Online named it the Best Documentary of 2004. To wrap up a year of awards and accolades, *Super Size Me* received an Academy Award nomination in the Best Documentary category.

Spurlock's first book, *Don't Eat This Book*, hit stores in May 2005 and picked up where the movie left off, diving even deeper into the psyche of a super-sized nation. His second TV series, *30 Days*, is set to premiere on the F/X Network in

## HOMETOWN
### West Virginia
#### BECKLEY

Photo: Avi Gerver

June 2005, and this fall he'll deliver the irreverent and topical social comedy *Public Nuisance* to the masses on Comedy Central.

Spurlock currently lives in the East Village in New York City with his Vegan fiancé, Alexandra Jamieson, and their manly cat, Sue.

OPPOSITE, TOP ] Promotion for *Super Size Me.*

ABOVE ] Spurlock weighing in for *Super Size Me.*

## FROM THE SOUL

For the first year after I left West Virginia, I was embarrassed to tell people where I was from. Their eyes would roll. They would laugh and make fun of my accent. I was an instant, walking punchline – the incarnation of every hillbilly joke they'd ever told and *Deliverance* come alive.

It was not until I met a man named Jake Jarrell, a fellow West Virginian who had worked in Hollywood for years, that my mind began to change. He took me under his wing and gave me some great down home advice: "If you just remember where you come from and what that means, you'll do great in this business. There aren't many people like us. Don't forget that."

My dad used to tell me, "There are two kinds of people in this world, those who do what they say they're going to do and everyone else." I grew up in a house where your word meant everything. If you started something, then by God you finished it. Your word was trust and others put trust in your words. It's a simple idea: Say what you mean and mean what you say. A parable that seems lost in many corners of the the world, but one that I try to exemplify every day. A trait born and bred in West Virginia.

We are strong willed, loyal, trustworthy people. Folks who work hard and expect others to do the same. Failure is not a part of our vocabulary, but humility is. And for me, there is an indescribable inspiration that flows steadily forth from the mountains that raised me into who I am today, for I truly am a creative product of the people and places that are "wild and wonderful."

Jake was right. There aren't many people like us...and I kind of like it that way.

# Clyde Ware

I was born in Clarksburg, West Virginia, at St. Mary's Hospital – which is long gone – and raised in West Union, thirty miles away, mainly by my maternal grandparents, Jim and Lucy Scott.

My parents, Clyde and Mary Scott Ware, were divorced when I was in third grade, as my father went to prison. Indications were that he was innocent of the charges, as his law-partner was a state senator and president of the bank in West Union who had dad "take the fall," promising him great things and assuring him that he wouldn't get a guilty verdict.

My granddad was injured in the oil fields in the 1930s and, after a long and painful recovery, the only work he could find during the Depression was as a janitor at Doddridge High School. I had to work cleaning up the high school with granddad at night and attend it during the day. I was always writing stories, as I would complete my schoolwork ahead of time and have nothing to do. That started my writing career. At the age of 11, I wrote my first play, *Stolen Blueprints*, and put it on for the grade school and high school.

After one year at WVU, on a scholarship, my grandparents' house was lost in the flood, along with all of my clothes. I couldn't go back to work at high school, so I went to work in the steel mills in Ohio. All the time I was continuing to write and finally saved up $100 to go to New York and *try*.

In New York I usually had three jobs at the same time – on the New York Journal-American as a copyboy, as a truck driver and a concession attendant/coat checker at Broadway theaters. I decided if I hadn't sold any of my writing and couldn't earn a living doing it, that I'd become an outlaw by the age of 30. I was trying to be an actor as well as a writer and managed to study with Lee Strasberg for five years before going to Hollywood.

I had planned my first "heist," but fortunately managed to make my first sale, to CBS' *Robert Herridge Theater* before I reached 30 – barely. I married Kay Doubleday, who was also in Strasberg's class, and we had one son, Jud Scott Ware.

My play, *Only The Good*, premiered in 1960, and I met my second wife, Davey Davison, an intern at the theater. Davey and I had a daughter, Lee Ashby Ware, and lived and

# HOMETOWN
## West Virginia

### WEST UNION

My education in West Virginia, unfortunately, did not include any "artistic" courses, as they were unavailable at the time.

worked in Hollywood until our divorce in 1972. We lived in France for a year before the divorce, where I wrote my two novels, *The Innocents* and *The Eden Tree*.

A couple of years later, I married Charlotte Young of West Union, who I had met while I was "back home" making *No Drums, No Bugles*, which starred Martin Sheen. Coming to Hollywood, Charlotte was a highly sought-after model and worked with me as an actress in *Hatfields and McCoys*, which I wrote/directed for ABC and starred Jack Palance. We divorced in the mid-70s, and Charlie became a nurse. She is working today in Parkersburg at St. Joseph's Hospital.

From the 1960s through the 1980s, I wrote, directed and/or produced over 150 television shows, including *Gunsmoke*, *Bonanza* and *Knots Landing* and many feature films. In the 1990s and in the 21st Century, I've continued developing properties for the screen and hope to make films and television based in West Virginia for the remainder of my life and career. My original screenplay

*Blackwolf* was recently purchased by Dennis Haysbert of FOX-TV's *24* and is currently in development.

In the late '90s, I had a comic book, *Zamindar*, published by Comico Comics, and hope to develop it for the screen in the near future. I'm also working on another book, *Tracy and Hepburn Told Me...*, which I hope to have published in late 2005.

OPPOSITE, LEFT ] Ware and Earl Holliman.

ABOVE ] Ware and Martin Sheen.

RIGHT ] *The Eden Tree* (1971).

In high school and in grade school before that, I started writing plays and fiction stories out of boredom, because I had worked out the curriculum ahead of time.

In high school, I was encouraged by the librarian to "read, read, read" and pretty much read everything available there, and continued writing, putting on plays for the high school.

In 21st Century West Virginia, I see an effort to include "artistic" classes in various schools, but primarily on the college level.

Clyde Ware
AUTHOR OF "THE INNOCENTS"

# THE EDEN TREE
A COMPELLING NARRATIVE OF LIFE, AND LOVE'S CONFLICTS

I'm trying to help in that effort, along with Jesse Cole Johnson, who was a third-party candidate for governor in 2004, and expect to be in West Virginia over the upcoming years to encourage and do a "hands-on" program to help young people in the state who have an interest in the arts.

# Diane Curry

Metropolitan Opera mezzo soprano DIANE CURRY was born in 1938 to Ashton and Frances Curry in White Sulphur Springs, West Virginia. In high school, she excelled in music and band. Not only was she first clarinet and a glee club soloist at White Sulphur Springs High, but she was also first clarinet with the West Virginia All-State Band and a singer with the West Virginia All-State Chorus, each for two years. She was also very active in school plays and musicals, including an all girls version of Gilbert and Sullivan's *The Mikado!*

A graduate of Westminster Choir College, Princeton, New Jersey, earning both a Bachelor and Masters of Music degrees, as well as the Outstanding Alumni Award, Curry taught music at Eastern Baptist College, Philadelphia, and The University of Delaware before returning to Westminster where she taught voice for seven years. When she wasn't teaching, she was an active soloist, performing oratorio for local concert groups.

Living in New York City and commuting to Westminster, she studied voice with teacher, mentor and *Joy In Singing* founder, Winifred Cecil. Curry became an alto soloist at New York's historic Fifth Avenue Presbyterian Church and soon after made her Carnegie Hall and Town Hall concert debuts.

In the early 1970s, she joined the New York City Opera at Lincoln Center where she performed for nearly a decade. She quickly learned the differences between opera and concert singing, beginning with small mezzo soprano roles and swiftly graduating to leads. Curry made debuts with New York Philharmonic Symphony Orchestra, Lincoln Center; American Symphony, Carnegie Hall; Spoleto Festival, Italy; and Opern Haus Graz, Austria.

Miss Curry joined the Metropolitan Opera as a guest artist in 1984 and performed with its touring company. Her official house debut at the Met took place five years later. It is with the Met that Curry honed her specialization in Wagnerian mezzo soprano roles (the operas of Richard

## HOMETOWN
### West Virginia

#### WHITE SULPHUR SPRINGS

# FROM THE SOUL

Growing up in White Sulphur Springs, where manners, good behavior, personal responsibility, integrity and respect for others were a normal part of everyday life, was a grounding experience. White Sulphur High had a very good music program that made a difference in many kids' lives – we traveled to band festivals outside of Greenbrier County and competed. We were able to excel and "spread our wings" in good, creative ways. Music and the arts not only feed our minds, emotions and spirits, but also makes us more intelligent – brain cells actually grow! Kids need the inspiration of creativity, but they also need to be guided to be prudent in what they listen to, as sound is the most powerful medium we have. It penetrates the psyche, the soul and emotions in positive or negative ways more powerfully than anything else! It can uplift us, inspire us or pull us down and drive us crazy.

In these seemingly negative times we need to choose for ourselves and our children the highest and best of music and arts to keep us grounded and positive and on our right paths.

To be a professional classical musician has to be a life – a lifestyle – and everything else has to come second, at least for a time. But to wonderful, regular, "normal" people, music and the arts is a necessary adjunct for life – a balance, a stress reliever. It's a spiritual uplifting, an inspiration and just plain fun. Kids need to have a good, creative background to help them fulfill their own limitless possibilities and reach for their own individual dreams and stars. The arts help us know anything is possible if we allow ourselves to think so.

Wagner), as well as the operas of Strauss and Verdi. She has achieved distinction for her performances of a wide opera and concert repertoire in Europe, North and South America and Japan.

Still performing, studying and teaching, Curry is also the critically acclaimed mezzo soloist on the Grammy-award winning and Grammaphone (London) recording of the Verdi *Requiem* with Robert Shaw and the Atlanta Symphony. She has also recorded Burton's *Ariel Symphony*

(Peters International), excerpts of *Porgy & Bess* (Phillips) and a concert of Mezzo Arias with the Bavarian Radio Orchestra.

OPPOSITE, LEFT ] Curry in the title role of Bizet's *Carmen*.

ABOVE ] Portraying the role Azucena in Verdi's *Il Trovatore*.

TOP, RIGHT ] Performance in Verdi's *Ballo in Maschera* as Ulrica.

# Littly Jimmy Dickens

From his very humble beginnings in the tiny Raleigh County community of Bolt, West Virginia, came a man who has risen to the greatest heights in country music. He's known the world over, and his name is LITTLE JIMMY DICKENS. At just four feet-eleven inches tall, he is considered to be country music's foremost entertainer.

Born James Cecil Dickens on December 19, 1920, he began singing at a young age whenever and wherever he could in various talent contests. Jimmy's radio debut interestingly came not as a singer, but as an imitator as he actually imitated the sound of a rooster crowing to sign the station on the air. He later worked alongside fellow West Virginians the Bailes Brothers and Molly O'Day before striking out on his own.

After excelling in four years of dramatics in high school, Jimmy received a scholarship to attend West Virginia State University. He opted not to go and, instead, pursued a career in country music.

Following ten years of stints at radio stations in West Virginia, Indiana, Ohio, Kansas and Michigan, and with the help of Roy Acuff, Jimmy was invited to become a member of the Grand Ole Opry in 1948. Jimmy has been in Nashville ever since.

Jimmy signed with Columbia Records and recorded more than 200 songs. From the start with light-hearted, up-tempo songs like *Take An Old Cold Tater And Wait*, *Country Boy* and *A-Sleeping At The Foot Of The Bed*, the sound of Little Jimmy Dickens really caught on. Another Dickens sound really caught on, too – that of one of country music's finest balladeers. Tunes like *We Could*, *Take Me As I Am (Or Let Me Go)* and *Life Turned Her That Way* – now country standards – were all originally introduced by Dickens.

A tireless road warrior who for decades worked 300 nights a year, Little Jimmy Dickens became the first country music entertainer to circle the globe on a world tour in 1964.

And speaking of entertainers, Little Jimmy Dickens is in a league all his

## HOMETOWN
### West Virginia

### BOLT

own. He steals the show every time and when he gets done with an audience, there's generally nothing left. He always leaves them begging for more.

In 1983, the industry's highest honor came when Dickens was elected into the prestigious Country Music Hall of Fame.

After more than 60 years in the business, complete retirement is not in Jimmy's vocabulary. Most weekends you'll find him at the Grand Ole Opry when he's not out making limited personal appearances.

It would be hard to imagine what country music would have been like had it not been for Little Jimmy Dickens. Thankfully, none of us will ever have to contemplate that. Simply stated, he's one of the all-time greats that both West Virginia and the country music industry will always be proud of.

---

THE WHITE HOUSE

WASHINGTON

April 30, 1985

I am delighted to send greetings to the citizens of Bolt, West Virginia as you welcome home Little Jimmy Dickens.

This fine entertainer has made so many contributions to country music and brought so much enjoyment to many people. It was fitting that in 1983 he was inducted by his peers into the "Country Music Hall of Fame." He also became the first country music artist to completely circle the globe on a world tour. This included entertaining the troops in Vietnam. All Americans are gratified by his many years of entertainment and sacrifices for his fellowman.

Nancy and I send our best wishes to Little Jimmy Dickens and the fine citizens of Bolt.

Ronald Reagan

---

OPPOSITE, LEFT ] Little Jimmy performing at the Grand Ole Opry.

ABOVE ] A letter from President Reagan to the town of Bolt.

TOP, RIGHT ] Little Jimmy's high school graduation photo.

---

# FROM THE SOUL

My career ambitions might never have materialized if not for one particular teacher at Trap Hill High School in Surveyor, West Virginia. It was there that I was fortunate to meet a devoted drama and public speaking teacher by the name of Ella Davis Lang. She was a very special lady. During the summer, Miss Lang worked on Broadway plays in New York, and then shared that professional experience when she returned to her students in the fall.

Because of my size – they don't call me Little Jimmy Dickens for nothing – I looked much younger than many other students. Perhaps that's why Miss Lang took a special interest in me. She felt I had an aptitude for the stage and encouraged me to participate in the school's public speaking and drama courses. During my four years in high school, she taught me stage presence, posture and especially crowd eye control. Miss Lang emphasized always directing my eyes to the back of the theater. That way any member of the audience, no matter its size, could feel I was talking directly to them.

After graduation, Miss Lang encouraged me to go to New York. She felt certain I could gain some parts in plays. But I was in love with the guitar and began my show-business career at WJLS radio in Beckley, West Virginia. During my 70 years in country music, I have been honored to play the Grand Ole Opry and share various stages with great superstars from Hank Williams, Sr. to Martina McBride. Yet to this day, no matter where I perform, I am proud to say that I still benefit from what I learned from Miss Ella Davis Lang.

Jimmy Dickens

# Johnnie Johnson
## 1924-2005

Photo: The Associated Press

The "Father of Rock & Roll Piano," Grammy-nominated JOHNNIE JOHNSON performed for over 70 of his 80 years. He passed away just months prior to this book's publishing. While Johnson's legendary piano licks graced dozens of classic Rock & Roll recordings from the '50s, it took another 40 years for his voice to be etched in vinyl.

"I could play piano for a million people with no problem, but I was 'strick' with stage fright if I even opened my mouth to sing in front of three people," Johnnie said. "Keith Richards kept after me to sing, so when we co-wrote *Tanqueray* for our first CD, I decided, 'OK, I'll sing' – so he can see how bad I am. To my surprise, everyone liked it!" That album, produced by Richards, was entitled *Johnnie B. Bad.*

On Johnnie's second CD, *Johnnie B. Back*, he sang on half of the dozen tracks. Accompanying the Johnnie Johnson Band were album guests Buddy Guy, Al Kooper, John Sebastian, Phoebe Snow, Max Weinberg and Steve Jordan. Said Johnnie, "I think I put more into this CD than the others...each CD I make brings me closer to being more comfortable in the studio, more comfortable singing, more better being me."

Johnnie Johnson was born in 1924 in Fairmont, West Virginia. His first taste of ivory was at age five when his mother bought an upright piano. "As soon as the piano came in, I sat down and just started playing it. My mother cried 'It's a gift from God' that I could just sit down and start playing," said Johnnie. "From there on then, wherever I was, I always had me a piano and a band."

# HOMETOWN
## West Virginia

### FAIRMONT

JOHNSON BIOGRAPHY CONT'D

After graduating high school in 1942, Johnnie moved to Detroit to work at the Ford Motor Company plant. A year later, he was drafted and served in the Marines as part of a special weapons crew in the South Pacific. "I stayed for 31 long months, traveling island to island, but even there I had a band. I played in our company's band, The Barracudas, and behind Bob Hope, Betty Hutton, Joe Stafford and lots of comedians. That's when I decided music was for me."

In 1946, Johnnie ended his tour of duty and returned to Detroit. "It was at this time that I heard T-Bone Walker – a guitar player playin' the blues. I was playing jazz at the time, and this was my first real introduction to it. He really influenced my sound." Johnnie then moved to Chicago for its hot music scene. He arrived on a Tuesday and was playing by Friday and over the years got to sit in with Muddy Waters, Howlin' Wolf, Little Walter, Memphis Slim, Etta James and the Moonglows.

In 1952, Johnnie moved to St. Louis. That New Year's Eve, scheduled to play a party, his saxophonist called in

sick. Johnnie quickly hired an 'unknown' named Chuck Berry. "Chuck's music raised all kinds of eyebrows that night because they weren't used to seeing a black man playing hillbilly music. We became the hottest band on the local scene and two or three years later Chuck took a tape of an old fiddle tune called *Ida Red* to Chicago's Chess Records. I changed the music and re-arranged it, Chuck re-wrote the words, and the rest, as they say, was history. Leonard Chess asked me to record it live. At that time, someone else had a song out by the same name, so we had to change our version. We noticed a mascara box in the corner, so we changed the name to *Maybellene*."

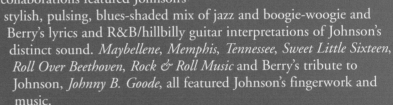

OPPOSITE, TOP ] Johnson's 2001 induction into the Rock & Roll Hall of Fame, pictured with fellow inductee James Burton and presenter Keith Richards.

The Johnson/Berry union created an infectious groove that transformed popular music and influenced a generation of musicians. Their collaborations featured Johnson's stylish, pulsing, blues-shaded mix of jazz and boogie-woogie and Berry's lyrics and R&B/hillbilly guitar interpretations of Johnson's distinct sound. *Maybellene, Memphis, Tennessee, Sweet Little Sixteen, Roll Over Beethoven, Rock & Roll Music* and Berry's tribute to Johnson, *Johnny B. Goode*, all featured Johnson's fingerwork and music.

Johnnie was recognized for his pioneering contribution to Rock & Roll in the acclaimed 1988 film "rockumentary," *Hail! Hail! Rock & Roll.* "I realized how important he was on Chuck's early records," said Keith Richards, "how his influence affected Chuck and how little credit he got for it at the time." Johnnie can also be seen as a featured artist on the PBS television special, *A Tribute to Muddy Waters*, taped at the Kennedy Center in Washington D.C.

Although it came late in his career, Johnnie was eventually truly embraced by the fans, press and the music community. He has received numerous awards and accolades, including a Congressional Citation, a Rhythm & Blues Foundation Pioneer Award and a Pioneer in Jazz Award from the New School University. His birthtown of Fairmont has instituted the Johnnie Johnson Jazz & Blues Festival. However, his shining moment came in 2001 when Johnnie was finally given his rightful place in the Rock & Roll Hall of Fame.

In the words of Johnnie's guitarist Tom Maloney: "Fairmont, West Virginia, is definitely an important part of Johnnie. He could have been born in New York, Chicago, Houston, St. Louis, or any other place in the world, but we wouldn't have Johnnie or Rock & Roll music as we know it today. Fairmont should be very, very, proud of Johnnie."

# Chester Lester

A GOOD NIGHT'S LOVE

CHESTER LESTER was born in Mammouth, West Virginia, a small coal mining town about sixty miles from Charleston. The family later moved to Tyler Mountain where he attended Cross Lanes Elementary School and, later, Nitro High School. He found interest in music in the seventh grade. By his freshman year in high school, he began to form several bands and played high school dances and roller-skating rinks.

While working night clubs in and around Beckley and Oak Hill, he met one of the State's best guitar players, Norman Chapman. Being somewhat older, Norman had worked with Nashville stars and local recording artist Eddie Seacrist on a TV show called *Pieces of Eight*. At the time Chester met him, he was working with *The Buddy Starcher Show* on WCHS. Buddy needed a bass player and vocalist and Norman recommended Chester. He worked with Buddy from 1963 until the show's end in 1967. The show not only exposed him to people in surrounding states, but also in Nashville, due to a syndicated show they did for an insurance company in that city. This offered Chester the opportunity to have his first recordings, *Patches, I'd Rather Switch than Fight* and *Any Place But Here* on Buddy's label. During this time, the show's band either worked package shows with, or backed up, Nashville recording artists such as Mel Tillis, Johnny Paycheck, Charlie Louvin, Hoyt Axton and many others. It was then that Chester began seriously thinking about going to Nashville.

After the show ended, Chester went on the road for two years with a local band. In his off time, Chester started writing songs. While on the road, his wife was sending his songs to Tommy Jennings, brother of Waylon Jennings, in Nashville. While he was working in Bowling Green, Kentucky, Chester made a trip to

# HOMETOWN
## West Virginia

### MAMMOUTH

Nashville and met Tommy. This gave him an open door in Nashville, as well as someone to help him with his songs. The band left the road and Chester started working in a Charleston club with one of the city's top night club performers, George Legg. Through this period of time, he kept writing his songs and in 1975 decided to make the move to Nashville. A fellow West Virginian, Russ Hicks, who had a publishing company with other steel guitar players Buddy Emmons and Jimmy Crawford, helped him in the move. He continued to write and demo his songs while playing bass for several bands. In 1979 Chester met Don King at Con Brio Records. Don took him to the label's owner, Bill Walker, and Bill signed Chester as a writer and recording artist. It was here he had his first two major recordings as an artist: *Mama Make Up My Room* and *If Only We Could*.

In 1982 Chester was introduced to Bob Montgomery at House of Gold Music and had his first major cuts as a songwriter, *He's the Fire* by Diana, and *Bedtime Stories* by Jim Chestnut. He was then signed as a staff writer

and had his first number one record *She Left Love All Over Me* by Razzy Bailey. These hits were followed with cuts by Con Hunley, Dean Martin, Joe Stampley, Mark Grey, Razzy Bailey, Waylon Jennings, Tammy Wynette, Bobby Vinton and several others. In 1989 Chester formed his own publishing company, Chester Lester Music, and had cuts by Waylon Jennings, Willie Nelson, Tammy Wynette and Johnny Cash. His Johnny Cash song, *Going by the Book*, was nominated for a Dove Award. During this time, he started producing sessions for artists from other countries. In 1995 he produced an album on Frank Jensen, which was the album of the year in the Netherlands. He is presently producing artists in the overseas market as well as recording himself overseas.

OPPOSITE, TOP ] (l-r) Lester on *The Buddy Starcher Show; A Good Night's Love* recorded by Tammy Wynette, words and music by Chester Lester.

TOP, RIGHT ] Lester appearing in Danish newspaper (1989).

# FROM THE SOUL

To be a songwriter, the first requirement is to have a very active imagination and to have the ability to paint pictures with words. This is how I believe my West Virginia education helped me.

It was the mid-1950s, my 6th grade class at Cross Lanes Elementary. Once a week, the teacher would pull down the shades to darken the room, turn on the radio and we would lay our heads on the desk. What came next was a voice from the PBS station saying, "This is West Virginia History on the air." We listened to how the Native Americans lived and learned about the burial mound in South Charleston. We listened in awe about the early settlers and their journeys up and down the Kanawha River. We knew that we loved our beautiful mountains, but now we knew how they were formed. Afterwards, we were told to draw a picture of what we saw based on what we'd heard.

I already had an active imagination, being surrounded by West Virginia's beautiful hills and mountains, but I believe this class helped me to develop it even more. It was through this simple radio show, which lasted no more than half an hour each week, that I learned pictures could be drawn from words…that imagination could be brought to life!

*Chester A. Lester*

# Kathy Mattea

KATHY MATTEA can look at her 20-year career and make a profound statement: "I am exactly where I want to be."

The West Virginia native came of age musically in the Nashville songwriting community, where she sang demos for rising young tunesmiths. Signed to her first recording contract in 1983, she nurtured that connection, giving a score of now-famous songwriters their first hit – and many their first #1. The list includes Nanci Griffith, whose *Love At The Five and Dime* was Mattea's first hit in 1986.

Her recordings brought attention to such diverse talents as Guy and Susanna Clark, Gillian Welch, Tim O'Brien and her husband, Jon Vezner. She also made unusual yet prescient choices when hiring musicians for her records and her band. She hired many musicians who went on to great acclaim as instrumentalists, including banjoist Bela Fleck, fiddler Mark O'Connor, bassist Edgar Meyer and guitarist Vince Gill (years before he became a household name). She often blended renowned veterans with these upstarts, using Nashville players, as well as such non-country talents.

It all came together to create a one-of-a-kind sound that set Mattea apart from her country music peers. She began to meet and collaborate with a wide range of artists from folk, bluegrass and Celtic backgrounds and forged a reputation as a thoughtful performer with a healthy growing edge. She began to amass a fiercely loyal fan base, and began to set herself apart as a respected artist both inside and outside the country music community.

She wasn't an instant star: she didn't have her first Top 10 hit until her eighth single. But once she found her true voice, she became one of country music's most distinctive and critically acclaimed artists. She's won two Grammy Awards, two Country Music Association (CMA) Female Vocalist of the Year awards, and her song *Eighteen Wheels And A Dozen Roses* was named CMA Single of the Year in 1998.

Mattea made the best of the leverage that success allowed her. Her albums always owned an adventuresome quality, from the rollicking acoustic sounds of *Untasted Honey* and *Lonesome Standard Time* to the Celtic influences of *Time Passes By* and *Love Travels* to the rockin' sound of *Walking Away A Winner*.

In 2000 she released her critically acclaimed album *The Innocent Years*, her last for Mercury Records. After 17

# HOMETOWN
### West Virginia

## CROSS LANES

years and a difficult corporate merger, Mattea asked to be released from her contract. With her freedom in hand, Mattea and her manager plotted their next move. Continuing along a path away from the Nashville Music Machine she considered small, major and independent labels, licensing agreements and even starting her own record company. She ended up signing with Narada Records, which had recently been purchased by Virgin Records. Well-known and respected as a jazz, world and contemporary instrumental music label, Narada gave Mattea the freedom to be unique and to explore new directions with her music.

For Mattea, it's the process as well as the result that's important. She is delighted with her current situation. She has a five-piece band that inspires and pushes her, and she works with people she respects. "My show is still evolving, and my fellow musicians challenge me to evolve as a singer, writer, player and performer. I still feel inspired about music. I am incredibly blessed."

ABOVE ] Cover of Kathy's 2002 release *Roses*.

PHOTOS: Russ Harrington

# FROM THE SOUL

I discovered choir and a love for singing in the 7th grade. I found other kindred spirits there, and began to find myself. The next year, I started band and discovered that moment where the group of us, just regular kids, crossed the line from the chaos, the cacophony of stabbing through the notes on the page, to something resembling music. It was the light bulb of realizing that my little French horn "voice" could contribute to something much larger than myself…the exhilaration of that synergy. Like discovering magic.

All-State Chorus just added to the fire. I remember one night, on the road in a two-story motel, we were all hanging out with our doors open, taking in the scene, and somehow, spontaneously, we all just came out to the 2nd story rails of the motel and began singing our repertoire – a capella. We were able to bestow – and experience for ourselves – a gift we had no power to manifest on our own. Like being plugged in to something much larger. It was the sheer joy of youth, of singing for its own sake. More magic.

In the years that have followed, through engineering and chemistry classes at WVU to my "day jobs" in Nashville, music has been the thread that has consistently connected me to the mystery of being separate, yet connected to others on this planet. The seeds were planted early. I was blessed by the arts in my school system. They kept me from being identified as "the brainy kid." They helped add balance to my life, and a sense of work and play happening at the same time. I will be ever-grateful to those that passed that gift on to me, and I cannot say enough how important the arts were in my school curriculum.

*Kathy Mattea*

# Charlie McCoy

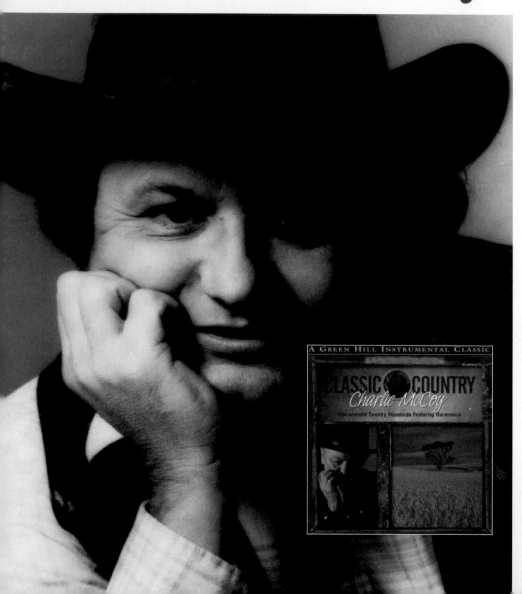

There are numerous super-session musicians in Nashville, but very few with the longevity of CHARLIE McCOY. In addition to being a fixture in Nashville studios for nearly four decades, he also has his own recording career, having released 28 albums in the last 32 years.

Charlie McCoy began working sessions in the early '60s, one of the first being on Roy Orbison's hit, *Candy Man*. "Forty-nine dollars," says McCoy. That's how much he was paid for that session back in 1961. "It got Roy another hit and me a career, and for a 20 year-old to make $49 for three hours work back then, it was a dream."

Shortly after the release of *Candy Man*, Charlie McCoy became one of the in-demand session players in Nashville. His session credits are literally a who's who of country music, doing upwards of 400 sessions per year. Charlie has since cut his session appearances down in the last few years to provide more time to tour in Europe and Japan, as well as the U.S.

In addition to his country sessions, Charlie McCoy was a mainstay on Elvis Presley recordings both in Nashville and Los Angeles. When Bob Dylan recorded *Blonde On Blonde*, *Nashville Skyline* and *John Wesley Harding* in Nashville, Charlie was one of the few Music City session players on those dates.

In his book *Backstage Pass*, Al Kooper described a typical Charlie McCoy incident that took place during the sessions for Dylan's *Blonde On Blonde* album. One song called for a trumpet part, something that should have been an easy overdub. However, Dylan didn't care for overdubs. So McCoy, while playing bass with his left hand, played trumpet with his right without missing a beat. Kooper

# HOMETOWN
### West Virginia

FAYETTEVILLE

## FROM THE SOUL

My first influences of beauty were of the New River Gorge and surrounding countryside. As a musician, I draw from all sources of inspiration. West Virginia is one of my main sources.

pointed out that Dylan stopped…in sheer amazement…during the middle of the recording.

Charlie McCoy began recording for Monument Records in the late '60s and recorded 12 albums for the label, beginning with *The Real McCoy* in 1969. He has been nominated and received so many awards over the years that it's hard to keep up with them. For instance, he's won a Grammy Award, two Country Music Association Awards and eight Academy of Country Music Awards.

While Charlie is predominately known as a harmonica player (he endorses the Hohner brand), his musical prowess encompasses most instruments, including guitar, bass, drums and keyboards, as well as a variety of wind and brass instruments. He served as the music director for the hit syndicated TV show *Hee-Haw* for 19 years.

After the demise of Monument Records in 1982, Charlie was without any record company affiliation for about five years. He and his band

recorded an album entitled *One For The Road* in 1986. Charlie has had three albums released in the United States on Step One Records and a gospel album on the Simitar label.

Charlie was presented the Musician award from R.O.P.E. in 1994, elected to the German-American Country Music Federation Hall of Fame in 1998 and to the Hall of Fame of the North American Country Music Association International in 2000. A consummate musician, as well as a caring person, Charlie McCoy is still inspired and is still very much *harpin'*.

OPPOSITE, TOP ] Charlie with Roy Clark on *Hee-Haw*.

OPPOSITE, INSET ] Charlie's latest release *Classic Country*.

TOP, RIGHT] Charlie performing with Ray Charles.

Charlie's legendary studio work can be heard across the board of musical styles on a number of classic recordings. Here's a selected sample of songs and albums that feature his amazing harmonica playing:

Bob Dylan: Five albums, including *Blonde On Blonde*
Chet Atkins: *Chet Picks On The Beatles*
Conway Twitty: *Play, Guitar Play*
Dolly Parton: *My Tennessee Mountain Home*
Elvis Presley: Seven movie soundtracks
George Jones: *He Stopped Loving Her Today*
Gordon Lightfoot: *Canadian Railroad Trilogy*
Jerry Lee Lewis: *What Made Milwaukee Famous*
Johnny Cash: *Orange Blossom Special*
Loretta Lynn: *When The Tingle Becomes A Chill*
Manhattan Transfer: *Love For Sale*
Nancy Sinatra: *Jackson*
Perry Como: *Dream On Little Dreamer*
Ringo Starr: *Beaucoup of Blues* album
Simon and Garfunkel: *The Boxer*
Steve Miller Band: *Going Back To The Country*
Tanya Tucker: *Delta Dawn*
Waylon Jennings: *Only Daddy That'll Walk The Line*

# Brad Paisley

Courtesy Country Music Assoc.

Born in the Ohio River town of Glen Dale, West Virginia, BRAD PAISLEY seemed destined for a life of music. When he was eight, his grandfather gave him his first guitar – a Sears Danelectro Silvertone with an amp in the case. By the age of ten, Paisley was playing well enough to accompany himself and soon began singing in church and at civic meetings. He formed his first band, Brad Paisley & the C-Notes, with his guitar instructor, local musician Clarence "Hank" Goddard. At twelve, Paisley wrote his first song, *Born on Christmas Day.* His junior high school principal heard it and asked him to play it at the next Rotary Club meeting. In the audience that day was Tom Miller, program director for WWVA, Wheeling's country radio powerhouse.

Miller was so impressed by the performance that he invited Paisley to make a guest appearance on Jamboree USA, the station's legendary Saturday night show. Paisley was ecstatic, and his performance went over so well that he was asked to become a regular. During his eight years on the show, he opened for such country luminaries – and personal favorites – as Roy Clark, Jack Greene and Little Jimmy Dickens.

Paisley's Jamboree membership also earned him the opportunity to perform each year at the outdoor summer festival, Jamboree in the Hills. The event routinely boasted dozens of top country acts and drew crowds of 60,000 or more. But the weekly Jamboree turned out to be Paisley's most valuable training ground. On the weekends he didn't perform, he would hang out backstage, soaking up tips from veteran performers like George Jones.

After high school, Paisley began his studies at nearby West Liberty College. But his college advisor, Jim Watson, urged him to move to Nashville and enroll in the Belmont University music business program.

At Belmont, Paisley met Frank Rogers, who now serves as his producer; Kelley Lovelace, a frequent songwriting partner; and many of the musicians who would later work in his band and play on his first album.

Paisley served his college internship at ASCAP, the performing rights association, where he met Chris DuBois, another of his co-writers. His friends at ASCAP set up an appointment with EMI Music

# HOMETOWN
### ▬ West Virginia ▬

### GLEN DALE

## FROM THE SOUL

Publishing. A week after graduation, Paisley signed a songwriting deal with the company.

Paisley earned extra money in Nashville by singing and playing on demos. One of these attracted the attention of Arista Nashville's A&R Department. After a series of meetings and phone calls, Paisley added his name to the Arista roster.

The newcomer made his mark in 1999 with the single *He Didn't Have to Be*, co-written with Lovelace. The song gave Paisley his first #1 single and helped his debut album *Who Needs Pictures* go platinum.

In 2000, Paisley won the Country Music Association's Horizon Award and the Academy of Country Music's best new male vocalist trophy and received his first Grammy nomination in 2001 in the all-genre best new artist category. He made his Grand Ole Opry debut in 1999 and, after 40 plus appearances, was inducted into the Opry on February 17, 2001.

In 2002, he released the album *Part II*, which garnered his third #1 hit, the hilarious *I'm Gonna Miss Her (The Fishing Song)*. His third album, *Mud on the Tires*, arrived in 2003 and its title track gave Pailsey his fourth #1 single. The album topped Billboard's Country charts and also includes the song *Whiskey Lullaby*, featuring Alison Krauss. The song won two Country Music Association Awards and two Academy of Country Music Awards in 2005.

Brad is married to actress Kimberly Williams-Paisley of ABC-TV's *According to Jim*. They make their home in Nashville.

OPPOSITE ] Paisley performing at the Opry. (Photo: Chris Hollo, courtesy of Grand Ole Opry Archives.)

OPPOSITE, INSET ] Paisley accepting a 2004 CMA Award.

TOP, RIGHT ] Paisley, age 12, on the grounds of West Virginia's State Capitol.

What I love about West Virginia is that it's a state full of small, "down to earth" towns. It's because of that very thing that I was able to receive special attention from my mentors and role models. Whether that was a grade school teacher or a local guitar hero, I always got the feeling that I was important to them.

This was very evident as I started out as a young guitar player in the Ohio Valley. My early guitar hero – Clarence "Hank" Goddard – was not only my guitar teacher, but he also helped me start my first band. He would beam with pride watching me on stage and continued to support me into my years of playing at Wheeling's historic Jamboree USA. The Jamboree staff band was made up of some of the best local musicians, all veterans, and still they took it upon themselves to show me the ropes. They took me on the road with them – these were my first times on tour – and really tried to educate me about the road and what music means to the people that you play for. The guitar players in the band, Zane Baxter and Roger Hoard, always gave me respect and guidance. They talked to me as an equal, even though looking back I was really green. I think that had everything to do with the West Virginia ideology that says everyone has worth. My hometown, my church and my schools always turned out to support my performances, and by doing so, gave me the confidence to move away and pursue my dreams.

I'm not sure I would have had that confidence or the experience necessary to do this at this level if I had been from a different place. I owe my hometown of Glen Dale and my home state of West Virginia almost everything.

# Squire Parsons

The Kingsme[n]

SQUIRE PARSONS, a native of West Virginia, was raised in a Christian home and was introduced to gospel music as a baby by his parents. His father, Squire Parsons, Sr., was a choir director in their home church and taught shaped note gospel music.

Squire attended West Virginia Institute of Technology, where he earned a Bachelor of Science degree in music in 1970. He has served as interim music director, church soloist, elementary school music teacher, high school band director and, in 1975, became the baritone singer for the Kingsmen Quartet. In 1979, Squire went into solo ministry.

In addition to being one of America's best loved soloists, Squire is a prolific songwriter. In 1981, his song *Sweet Beulah Land* was voted Favorite Song of the Year by the Singing News.

# HOMETOWN
### West Virginia

NEWTON

## FROM THE SOUL

Some of the other gospel classics written by Parsons include: *Master Of The Sea, Oh What A Moment, The Broken Rose, He Came To Me, I Call It Home, I Sing Because, Hello Mama, I'm Not Giving Up* and *I Go To The Rock*. Many gospel recording artists and groups have recorded at least one of his songs.

In 1999, Squire was honored by his alma mater, West Virginia Institute of Technology, with an honorary Doctorate of Humanities.

Since 1979, Squire has performed an average of 200 dates per year at many churches and other venues. He has been a part of the *Singing At Sea* cruise and the *January Bible Study* cruise with Templeton Tours of Boone, North Carolina, since 1975. Squire and his wife, Linda, have also co-hosted over 20 trips to Israel. He has also been a part of the very popular *Gaither Homecoming* video series.

Squire was ordained at his home church, Trinity Baptist, in Asheville, North Carolina, in 1979. He and Linda live in Leicester, North Carolina. They have four adult children.

OPPOSITE, TOP ] Parsons with The Kingsmen in 1977.

TOP RIGHT ] Parsons teaching band and choir at Hannan High School of Mason County, WV (1971); and his Silver Anniversary Collection (1999).

Through the elementary, secondary and undergraduate programs of West Virginia, combined with the dedication of inspiring educators, I was given the tools to be able to develop my God given talents of performance and composing, which enabled me to more confidently present them to many varied audiences.

My music education started in my childhood home with my parents and family. My father, Squire Parsons, Sr., taught us to sing in the traditional shaped note music style. This style of music kindled my interest in music, which then was further fanned by Dr. Carl Brown and Ed Vineyard at Spencer High School. West Virginia Institute of Technology, presently West Virginia University Institute of Technology, was where my passion was fully ignited by Professors Don Riggio, Dr. Charles Martin and most of all, my mentor, encourager and vocal instructor, Professor Guy Owen Baker.

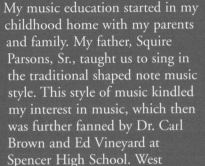

• featuring "Sweet Beulah Land" •

Squire parsons

# Rachel Proctor

BNA Records newcomer RACHEL PROCTOR just might be the most seasoned pro you've ever met. With one listen to her debut album, *Where I Belong*, you hear the enormous musical diversity in her background. But although she sings a variety of styles well, Rachel knows exactly where she belongs.

"I was never completely happy doing any other styles, because I always sang country music growing up," says the Charleston, West Virginia, native. "I really started focusing on country when I was 17 and I thought, 'Oh man, this is cool.' Almost immediately, I started making trips back and forth to Nashville."

The daughter of a nursing assistant and a supermarket manager, Rachel Proctor has been performing full time since age 6. When she was in the second grade, her teacher noticed that she wouldn't sing along with the other children.

"My grandma came down and said, 'Oh honey, why aren't you singing? You've got to sing. This is part of your grade.' I went, 'Oh no. My voice wiggles when it comes out,' because I had a vibrato even then. And that sounded different from everybody else, so I wouldn't sing. And that's how they figured out that I could."

Her grandma taught her to sing Dolly Parton's *I Will Always Love You* shortly thereafter. And her advice was always the same: "Sing it with feeling!"

Photo: Kristan Barlowe

When Rachel was in the fourth grade she appeared in a local production of the musical *Annie*. A year later came *The Sound of Music*. She competed in the talent portions of dozens of beauty pageants as a kid, just for the experience.

"When I was 17 and a senior in high school, a local band called me and asked me to start fronting the group because they had lost their female singer. What they did was all country. So suddenly I was singing Patty Loveless songs, Kelly Willis songs, just wonderful things. And loving it."

Rachel Proctor honed her country style in the clubs, Moose Lodges, fairs and festivals of West Virginia. She was writing country songs by the time she graduated from high school and was

# HOMETOWN
## ━━ West Virginia ━━
### CHARLESTON

making trips to Nashville to peddle them by age 18.

Rachel's band, 40 West, competed on the same circuit as Rob Byus's band, Full House. One night, when he was watching her perform, he turned to his friend and said, "I'm going to marry that girl."

"When I got the call from Nashville about getting my first song-publishing deal, I had just met Rob. We had known each other maybe a month and all I could think about was, 'Oh, I can't move to Nashville. I can't leave Rob.' My mom said, 'Rachel Christine Proctor, you get your stuff packed! You are going!' So Rob came with me and we got married a few months later."

Back then, Blake Shelton, Rob and Rachel were all struggling unknowns, touring in a band together to keep bread on the table. Rachel's initial attempts to get a recording contract in 1995 had all been met with rejections, and after about five years together, the couple divorced in Music City in 1999.

"Getting turned down makes you think about your focus. I think I was always following trends, thinking about what sounds good on the radio now and wanting to do that. I know the reason that wasn't working was because that wasn't me. I should have had the attitude: 'This is what I do. You like it or you don't.' Plus, I got divorced and had to grow up a little bit. I was going through being separated from Rob, trying to learn how to be independent, pay my own bills and do all that kind of stuff. But I was missing him, and so I started writing all these songs. And they were really concise, and I felt they were better than anything I had ever written."

OPPOSITE, LEFT] *Where I Belong* (2004).

PROCTOR BIOGRAPHY CONT'D

BNA Records, sister label to McBride's RCA label, asked to hear the new songs she'd been writing. The company had rejected her twice previously, so Rachel wasn't counting on anything. But the third time turned out to be the charm, and she signed with BNA Records, part of the RCA Label Group, in 2002.

Her debut album, *Where I Belong*, showcases her vocals, songwriting and musical diversity. The album includes the powerful single *Me and Emily*, and the wistful, quiet balladry of the title track. With its string quartet, pretty melody and contemplative tone, Rachel cites it as her favorite song on the CD.

Photo: Kristan Barlowe

"I feel like I have learned so much in Nashville. I can't imagine never having made the move. Singing is basically all I've ever done. There was nothing else for me to do, and nothing else I wanted to do."

# Buddy Starcher

1906-2001

Buddy Starcher, a radio entertainer who achieved tremendous popularity in his home state of West Virginia, enjoyed a long career in country music. While having only two hits of national consequence, he nonetheless managed to gain wide respect and influence among both fans and fellow artists.

Fans of the late Keith Whitley may recognize Starcher's name from the 1991 RCA album *Kentucky Bluebird*. The opening cut of the album features an undated segment taken from Starcher's popular morning show on WCHS-TV in Charleston, West Virginia, in which the pre-teen Whitley sings *You Win Again*.

---

*Oh! I love you my darling, how I love you*
*If I talk, will you try to understand*
*It's no matter how you treat me, I love you*
*And I'll still write your name in the sand.*

–Buddy Starcher, *I'll Still Write Your Name in the Sand*

---

Starcher was born March 16, 1906, near Ripley, West Virginia. He learned to play guitar under the tutelage of his father, an old-time fiddler. Starcher took his first job as a radio performer in 1928 at WFBR in Baltimore. He began writing his own songs – often about current events – and over the next several years worked at stations in Washington, D.C., North Carolina, Virginia, Iowa, Pennsylvania and his home state of West Virginia. Red Sovine, a fellow West Virginian, counted Starcher as one of his influences, as did other entertainers such as Mac Wiseman, Lee Moore, Sleepy Jeffers and Smiley Sutter.

Although he had been popular on radio for many years, Starcher didn't cut a record until 1946, when he did 16 sides for the Four Star label, including the best known of his early compositions: *I'll Still Write Your Name in the Sand*, a

# HOMETOWN
### West Virginia

KENTUCK

ABOVE ] Starcher with wife, Mary Ann, and cast on the set of his morning show on WCHS-TV in Charleston, West Virginia.

Top 10 hit in 1949. He did 10 more numbers for Columbia beginning in 1949, which included his own *Pale Welded Flower* and had a session for Deluxe in 1954. Buddy had several releases on Starday and recorded an album for them in 1962. Early in 1966, he did a recitation for the small Boone Record Company entitled *History Repeats Itself*. It became something of a surprise hit on both

the Country (Top 2) and Pop (Top 40) charts, leading Decca to buy the master and rush an entire Starcher album onto the market. It came as something of a shock to a 60 year-old with nearly 40 years of media experience.

In the early 1950s, Starcher turned from radio to television, working at outlets in Miami and Harrisonburg. In January 1960, he returned to Charleston and, for six years, had a highly rated early morning program on WCHS-TV. In addition to Buddy and his wife, Mary Ann, key figures in the show's success included comedian/vocalist Sleepy Jeffers, the Davis Twins, guitarist Norm Chapman, the lovely young gospel singer Lori Lee Bowles, comedian/steel player Herman Yarbrough and two young singers, Darius Ray Parsons and Chester Lester. This broadcast further contributed to Buddy's near legendary status in West Virginia and won him a new generation of fans in adjacent states, as well.

Other than *History Repeats Itself*, a clever comparison of Presidents Lincoln and Kennedy, Buddy Starcher has several noted songs to his credit. *I'll Still Write Your Name in the Sand* and *Fire in My Heart* became bluegrass classics through recordings by Mac Wiseman. Numerous artists have recorded Buddy's *Sweet Thing* since the Callahan Brothers first recorded it in 1941 and *A Faded Rose, A Broken Heart* were minor classics for both Hank Snow and Doc Williams. Starcher was also one of the first country singers to write an autobiography (in his well printed fan club journal, Starcher's Buddies, in 1944-1945), to have a published biography, *Bless Your Little Heart* in 1948 and, at the age of 80, to have a second biography (*Buddy Starcher Biography* by Robert Cagle), appear in print.

# Eleanor Steber

## 1916-1990

Cordial greetings
Eleanor Steber

The eminent American soprano, ELEANOR STEBER, grew up in a musical family. Her mother was an accomplished amateur singer who taught her daughter voice and piano, took her to concerts, arranged for coaching and strongly encouraged her to study and to sing in school and community shows. Eleanor later studied at the New England Conservatory in Boston, originally intending to major in piano. Her voice teacher, William Whitney, persuaded her to focus on singing. She received her Bachelor of Music degree in 1938.

In the beginning she did a lot of radio, oratorio and church work. Steber's opera debut was in 1936, appearing as Senta with the Commonwealth Opera in a production of Wagner's *The Flying Dutchman*, a demanding role indeed for a 21 year-old. In 1939, she went to New York to study with Paul Althouse, who had a great influence on her, and the following year, she won first prize at the Metropolitan Opera Auditions of the Air, earning a Met contract.

Eleanor Steber's first role at the Met was Sophie in Strauss' *Der Rosenkavalier* in October 1940. During the next years she benefited from conductors such as Bruno Walter, Sir Thomas Beecham, Erich Leinsdorf and George Szell. She was a versatile artist and appeared in Italian, French and German operas. Things began to change for her at the Met when Rudolf Bing took over the company in 1950.

By this time, her career extended well beyond New York to San Francisco, Chicago and Europe. Altogether she appeared 286 times in New York and 118 times on tour. She sang 28 leading roles in an extremely large repertoire.

Her easy upper range, coupled with a rich, smoothly produced lower voice made her a natural for Mozart roles, which she sang brilliantly. As her

voice matured, she sang some of the spinto roles in both the German and Italian repertoire. Steber was perhaps most famous for her creation of the title role in Samuel Barber's opera *Vanessa* and for commissioning his *Knoxville: Summer of 1915*.

Steber was one of the most important sopranos in the USA during the 1940s and 1950s, with a sweet, yet full, voice and outstanding versatility.

# HOMETOWN
### West Virginia

### WHEELING

Her recitals were practically vocal pentathlons for their wide range of styles and vocal demands. Her European engagements included appearances at Edinburgh (1947), Vienna (1953) and Glyndebourne. In 1953, she was the first American to appear at the Bayreuth Festival after the Second World War.

In addition to operas and recitals, Steber was a frequent guest on *The Voice of Firestone's* television broadcasts. After years of performing on stage, her voice had begun to show some wear; these television appearances helped extend her career.

Eleanor Steber was head of the voice department at the Cleveland Institute of Music from 1963 to 1972. She also taught at The Juilliard School in New York and at her alma mater, The New England Conservatory of Music. In 1975, she established the Eleanor Steber Music Foundation in order to assist young, professional singers. With R. Beatie, she published the study Mozart Operatic Arias in 1988. Her self-titled autobiography was published posthumously in 1992.

## SELECTED PERFORMANCES

Vanessa in
Samuel Barber's *Vanessa*

Marie in
Berg's *Wozzeck*

Fiordiligi in
Mozart's *Così fan tutte*

The Countess in
Mozart's *Le nozze di Figaro*

Pamina in
Mozart's *Die Zauberflöte*

Donna Anna in
Mozart's *Don Giovanni*

Konstanze in
Mozart's *Abduction from the Seraglio*

Arabella (the Met's first) in
Strauss' *Arabella*

Sophie in
Strauss' *Der Rosenkavalier*

Eva in
Wagner's *Die Meistersinger von Nürnberg*

Elsa in
Wagner's *Lohengrin*

Desdemona in
Verdi's *Otello*

# Billy Edd Wheeler

Born and raised in Boone County, West Virginia, BILLY EDD WHEELER graduated from Warren Wilson Junior College, Swannanoa, North Carolina, in 1953 and Berea College, Kentucky, in 1955. After service in the Navy's Air Force, he did graduate studies at Yale's School of Drama under John Gassner, majoring in playwriting. He has lived in Swannanoa since 1963, except for a stint managing United Artists Music Group in Nashville from 1968 to 1970. United bought his songwriting contract from legendary songwriter-publishers Jerry Leiber and Mike Stoller, then located in New York City.

Wheeler has received 13 awards from ASCAP for songs recorded by Judy Collins, Bobby Darin, The Kingston Trio, Johnny Cash, Neil Young, Kenny Rogers, Elvis and over 150 other artists here and abroad, selling over 60 million units. The songs include: *Jackson* (Grammy winner for Cash & Carter and a pop hit for Nancy Sinatra); *Blistered; The Rev. Mr. Black; Desert Pete; Anne; High Flying Bird; The Coming of the Roads; It's Midnight; Ode to the Little Brown Shack Out Back; Coal Tattoo;* and *Coward of the County*, which was a big hit for Kenny Rogers and was made into a movie.

Wheeler is author of a dozen plays, a folk opera commissioned by the National Geographic Society, *A Song of the Cumberland Gap*, and four outdoor dramas that include the long-running *Hatfields & McCoys* at Beckley, West Virginia, and *Young Abe Lincoln* at Lincoln City, Indiana. His new play, *Johnny Appleseed*,

premiered June 26, 2004, at Mansfield, Ohio, and was directed by Gerald Freedman of NYC theatre fame. Wheeler has authored or co-authored several books of humor, including *Laughter in Appalachia*, now in its 13th printing. August House Publishers recently made the claim that out of 599 books published over a 22-year period, *Laughter in Appalachia* is their best seller. *Real*

*Country Humor/Jokes From Country Music Personalities* was published in June, 2002. His novel, *Star of Appalachia*, was published in the fall of 2003.

Recently inducted into the Hall of Fame by Nashville Songwriters International, he is the recipient of Distinguished Alumnus awards from Warren Wilson College and Berea

# HOMETOWN
## West Virginia

WHITESVILLE

College. Other awards include Best Appalachian Poetry from Morris Harvey College, now the University of Charleston, West Virginia, and Billboard Magazine's Pacesetter Award for Music and Drama.

Married to the former Mary Mitchell Bannerman, the Wheelers have two children, Lucy and Travis, and continue to live in Swannanoa.

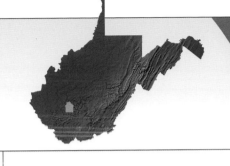

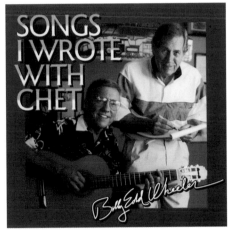

OPPOSITE, RIGHT] *Milestones* (2000)

ABOVE] (l-r) Induction into the Hall of Fame by Nashville Songwriters International; and *Songs I Wrote with Chet* (1995).

TOP, RIGHT ] Billy Edd in Charleston, West Virginia, to do radio and television promotion in the late 1960s; with Johnny Cash.

# FROM THE SOUL

I am honored to be included in Volume One of *Art & Soul: West Virginians in the Arts.*

I finished junior high school at Whitesville and attended Sherman High School in Seth, West Virginia, before attending Warren Wilson Junior College in Swannanoa, North Carolina, the place I now call home.

It was at Whitesville Junior High where I was first encouraged to "ham it up" on stage, and this continued at Sherman High. In one variety show I was asked to sing a Phil Harris song, a patter song, and I'm sure it was this experience that led to the writing of my first big hit, *The Rev. Mr. Black,* as recorded by The Kingston Trio.

While singing at the State Arts & Crafts Fair in Ripley, I was driven around to various communities to help promote the fair. At a Dairy Queen-type place, the owner paid me the highest compliment I've ever received. He said, "That's the song I want played over my grave when I die." To a creative person, such comments are worth more than money.

# Melvin Wine

## 1909-2003

West Virginia Traditional Life

# Goldenseal

Spring 1999    $4.95

## Vandalia Time!

Mother's Day

State Police

Clingman's Market

Courtesy Goldenseal Magazine

Photo: Mark Crabtree

Born in 1909 in Braxton County near Burnsville, West Virginia, fiddler MELVIN WINE'S inspiration and influence can be heard throughout the state and far beyond its borders.

Wine represented a living legacy of old-time musical traditions, playing music based on life's hard lessons and his personal experiences as a farmer, coal miner and father of ten. A very religious man, his style of playing was recognized the world over as one that held true to the styles of the 19th Century while maintaining a distinct central West Virginia repertoire. With a catalog of over

# HOMETOWN
### West Virginia

## BURNSVILLE

250 songs, his playing not only paid homage to traditional music, but also sustained it.

Wine was honored both regionally and nationally for his unique bowing skills. In 1981, he was the recipient of the very first Vandalia Award – West Virginia's highest folk-life honor – at the annual Vandalia Gathering held each summer on the grounds of the State Capitol in Charleston. The honor recognizes a lifetime

OPPOSITE, LEFT] Wine on the cover of West Virginia's *Goldenseal* Magazine (Spring 1999).

ABOVE] *Fiddling Way Out Yonder: The Life and Music of Melvin Wine* by Drew Beisswenger (2002).

contribution to the state and its traditional culture. A staple at the West Virginia Folk Festival in Glenville from the late '50s on, he was a constant winner of ribbons and new fans. Wine was also awarded the National Endowment for the Arts' prestigious National Heritage Fellowship in 1991, the highest recognition given to a folk artist in the United States. Upon acceptance of this award, Wine won the opportunity to perform in Washington, D.C.

Community, music and, perhaps most of all, tradition were Wine's biggest life influences. However, his biggest musical influence was his father. He took his influences and shared them with others, teaching student fiddlers at regional workshops and classes at the Augusta Heritage Center at Davis & Elkins College in Elkins, West Virginia. Through the West Virginia Folk Art Apprenticeship Program, Wine worked directly with three young fiddlers, sharing with them his alternate tunings, bowing techniques and his favorite keys.

In the summer of 2002, the biography *Fiddling Way Out Yonder: The Life and Music of Melvin Wine* was published by the University Press of Mississippi. Drew Beisswenger's book addresses the historical issues related to both North American fiddling and Wine's personal history, as well as his desire to communicate the spirit of his Braxton County home through music and to simply have an old-fashioned good time.

A sought-after fiddler with a seemingly endless supply of unique tunes and techniques, Melvin Wine passed away in March of 2003.

# Bill Withers

BILL WITHERS is one of America's premier singer/songwriters. Combining soulful warmth, a folksy, genuine feel and an immediately recognizable voice, Withers has sung his way into the hearts of millions. He has an uncanny ability to say with profound honesty and great sensitivity what so many of us feel in our hearts, but are unable to express in words.

His music and lyrics have a universal appeal, simple yet sophisticated. Bill attributes this to his own universality – as he describes it, a rural childhood and an urban-international adulthood.

Born in Slabfork, West Virginia, the youngest of six children in a small coal mining town, his youthful musical experiences were mainly in gospel quartets in small churches.

During a nine-year term in the Navy, which carried him throughout the Far East, Withers was inspired to try his hand at singing. Songwriting came as a result of futile searches for original songs that expressed what he felt.

After his discharge from the Navy, he moved to Los Angeles and recorded demos of his tunes in hopes of landing a recording contract. In 1971, signed to Sussex Records, came such memorable hits as *Ain't No Sunshine*, *Grandma's Hands* and in 1972, *Lean On Me* and *Use Me*. Later would come the striking *Lovely Day* and *I Want To Spend The Night*.

He was awarded Grammy Awards as a songwriter for *Ain't No Sunshine*, in 1971, and for *Just The Two of Us*, in 1981. In 1987, Bill received his ninth Grammy nomination and third Grammy as a songwriter for the re-recording of the 1972 hit *Lean On Me* by Club Nouveau. *Lean On Me* was re-recorded and performed at the 1992 Presidential Inauguration festivities by Michael Bolton.

# HOMETOWN
## West Virginia

### SLABFORK

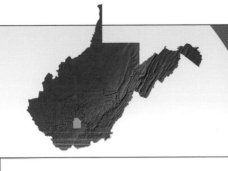

## FROM THE SOUL

Bill's songs have been recorded by hundreds of artists including Barbra Streisand, Michael Jackson, Liza Minelli, Aretha Franklin, Tom Jones, Linda Ronstadt, Joe Cocker, Johnny Mathis, Mick Jagger, Sting, Crystal Gale, Nancy Wilson, Carmen McCrae, Diana Ross, Grover Washington, Jr., Luther Vandross, Dave Braun and Boney James, to name a few.

Artists that have recorded music written by Withers cover genres such as pop, jazz, country and western, classical, rhythm and blues, gospel and hip-hop.

Bill's music and unique voice have been used in numerous television and radio commercials, motion pictures and television programs. His music has been sampled and covered by many hip-hop and rap artists of today, including Blackstreet and their composition *No Diggity;* Will Smith's version of *Just The Two Of Us;* and Black Eyed Peas' *Bridging The Gap.*

The recent Number #1 Pop and Country album by Jimmy Buffett surprisingly contains two songs by Bill Withers, one co-written with Mr. Buffett.

Bill has the gift of combining sincere melodies with common sense lyrics to evoke a human value. As one critic put it, "If life is one of experiences, who better than Bill Withers could put both the elements of music and words together that all relate to."

For Bill it is quite simply stated, "I write and sing about whatever I am able to understand and feel. I feel that it is healthier to look out at the world through a window than through a mirror. Otherwise, all you see is yourself and whatever is behind you."

OPPOSITE, TOP ] (l-r) *Just As I Am* (1971); *Still Bill* (1972); and *Menagerie* (1977).

If I am known or remembered for anything, hopefully it is for the words that I have written. Correction: co-written.

I say that because my co-writer has been and always will be my upbringing in the coal camps and the small towns in the hills of West Virginia. *Lean On Me* is a reflection of the West Virginia tradition of lending a hand to your neighbor. Even across racial lines in the segregated West Virginia of the 1930s, '40s and '50s when I grew up, whoever came across someone in need would more than likely lend a hand.

*Grandma's Hands* is a reflection not only of my own grandmother, but of all of the grandmothers who have watched over their own grandchildren and those of others from their swings and rocking chairs on porches throughout the state.

That social education and the fact that the West Virginia schools that I attended from 1944 through 1956 had English programs and dedicated teachers that imparted a facility for the language has enabled me to function professionally as a songwriter and publisher. That education and preparation has also enabled me to communicate both verbally and on paper well enough to function as a businessman and occasional public speaker.

To West Virginia Public Education in general: I owe you, I thank you.

Becky **Kelly**

*Lush green foliage,*

*textured mountains,*

*rolling hills. The scent*

*of green that lifts your*

*spirits...and fills your*

*heart with joy.*

*Honeysuckle drifting on*

*soft-as-feather breezes.*

*This is what I love*

*about West Virginia.*

BECKY KELLY creates a world seemingly suspended in time – a world where children dangle their toes in clear running streams...best friends giggle and daydream in the comfortable crook of an ancient tree...and ethereal fairies doze on dew-dappled leaves.

But Becky is quick to point out that what she paints is not fantasy. The scenes she paints are based on the real world – with just a sprinkling of stardust to add a bit of magic.

Becky draws on her past before she draws in her sketchbook. She has crystal-clear memories of her childhood spent in the Appalachian mountains of West Virginia, and this lush and beautiful landscape provides the backdrop for many of her enchanting watercolors. On walks through the woods, her father would always encourage Becky to keep a watchful eye out for fairies, spurring her imagination to fill in the details of what the shy little creatures might look like. Today, these fairies make frequent appearances in Becky's art.

Becky's paintings are also alive with the joyful sound of children at play. Her son, Payton, his friends, and even his stuffed animals have provided Becky with a constant source of inspiration for the past several years.

Always an artistic child, Becky began experimenting with watercolor painting in grade school. She fondly remembers accompanying her father, an architect and painter, on trips to the countryside where they would set up easels side-by-side and paint for hours. Becky won many local art competitions in high school and went on to study painting, illustration and design at the Columbus College of Art and Design in Ohio.

# HOMETOWN
## West Virginia

### ST. ALBANS

## FROM THE SOUL

After graduating, she accepted a position as an illustrator at Hallmark Cards in Kansas City, Missouri. Ultimately Hallmark built an entire line of greeting cards and gift-related products around her work; they called it *Spoonful of Stars.*

When her son Payton was born in 1992, Becky left the safe corporate world of Hallmark for the uncertainty of freelance to spend more time at home. Becky Kelly Studio was officially open for business.

Becky's work bloomed. Eventually she launched her own successful line of greeting cards and related products, under the Becky Kelly label.

Becky began licensing from a growing list of publishers anxious to use her illustrations. Most notably are her line *Enchanted Garden* and her baby lines, *My Little One* and *PJ and Friends.* Her work can be found in gift books, on prints, posters, baby books, photo albums, journals, teacups, nightshirts, baby room accessories and many other products.

Over the years she has been a frequent contributor to award-winning children's magazines like *Ladybug, Spider,* and *Weekly Reader.* She has also worked with educational publishers Scholastic, Grolier, Henry Holt and Brown, among others.

For those familiar with West Virginia, it is easy to see how the state's beautiful woodland forests and natural parks inspire Becky's art. Look closely at her work and you might recognize many of the lovely creeks and rolling hills of Greenbrier, or the magical wonders of the intertwining roots, rocks and trees of Bear town.

Visitors to the Culture Center in Charleston can see where Becky began her illustrating career with a summer college internship program with the West Virginia Library Commission. And the corner shop on Main Street in her hometown of St. Albans carries a wide range of Becky's cards, books and other products.

*www.beckykelly.com*

I must have driven my third grade teacher, Mrs. Stanley, nuts.

She'd ask me "Why did you stop writing mid-sentence?" "Why did you doodle all over your notebook?"

But even after many parent teacher conferences, fretting about me with my mother, Mrs. Stanley didn't give up on me. Instead, she embraced my creativity. She made me feel special and unique.

Years later at St. Albans High School, I encountered another amazing teacher. Mrs. Young made learning interesting. She was extremely creative in her assignments, and I couldn't wait to attend her classes. She, too, made me feel appreciated for my creativity.

But my very first teacher was my father, an architect who happens to also be an excellent watercolorist. As a child, I would follow my dad to set up easels in the countryside to paint side-by-side. With a pad of paper, brushes, watercolors and a gallon jug of water, he would teach me how to see light and shadow or how to create a tree with only a few quick brush strokes and a sharp knife. He taught me many of the techniques that I use today; that drawn lines are expressive and should be seen, and most importantly, that mistakes make art more interesting.

I will forever be grateful for the teachers that nurtured my creativity and made a career in art seem possible. West Virginia has so much to offer. The lush, boundless beauty of its landscapes are matched in magnificence only by the generous souls who dwell here — lifting and encouraging others. It's a great place to be a daydreamer.

*Becky Kelly*

# Blanche Lazzell
## 1878-1959

The modern artist BLANCHE LAZZELL was born on a small farm in Maidsville, West Virginia, in 1878. The second youngest of twelve children, Lazzell was educated at the one-room Lazzell School from the first through eighth grade. She enrolled in the West Virginia Conference Seminary (now West Virginia Wesleyan College) in 1894. Lazzell studied art at West Virginia University from 1901-1905, receiving a degree in fine arts. The artist continued her education by moving to New York and enrolling in the Art Students League in 1907 where she studied with William Merritt Chase. She traveled throughout Europe in 1912 and took classes in Paris at the Académie Julian and Académie Moderne. Lazzell moved to the art colony of Provincetown, Massachusetts, in 1915 where she would spend most of her professional career. It was in Provincetown that Lazzell learned the white-line technique for producing color woodcut prints, which are the much-respected base of her artistic reputation.

In 1923, at the age of forty-five, Lazzell returned to Europe to study with cubist artists André Lhote, Ferdand Legér and Albert Gleizes. During the Depression, Lazzell was employed by the Public Works of Art Project in West Virginia, creating a mural and four color woodblock prints. From 1936 to 1939 she produced 122 prints and paintings for the Works Progress Administration in Massachusetts. During this time, she joined German-born modernist Hans Hofmann's Provincetown drawing class. Hofmann was a legendary teacher of the modern principles in art to an American audience. Lazzell and Hofmann formed a friendship that lasted the rest of her life. With Hofmann's help, Lazzell was acknowledged as a pioneer of the modern art movement in America and was given an exhibition at Gallery 200 as part of the prestigious Forum '49. This was a summer-long series of lectures, discussions and exhibitions that foregrounded the new developments in contemporary art. Some of Lazzell's strongest abstractions date from the mid-1940s until her

# HOMETOWN
## West Virginia

### MAIDSVILLE

death in 1959. Throughout Lazzell's career, she was always searching for new ideas to incorporate into her artistic vision. In the end, it was that vision, along with her training, that made her a significant American artist.

Throughout her lifetime, Lazzell was included in many important national and international exhibitions. In 1919, she was one of eleven artists to participate in the first show of color woodblock prints by American artists at the Detroit Institute of Arts. In France, she was included in the prestigious Salon d'Automne from 1923-28 and in 1930, and in the L'Art D'Aujourd'hui Exposition Internationale. Back in America, she was exhibited in the First International Exhibition of Lithography and Wood Engraving at the Art Institute of Chicago, the Fifty Color Prints of the Year in Los Angeles, the PWPA exhibition at the Corcoran Gallery in Washington, D.C., and at the Museum of Modern Art in New York.

OPPOSITE, LEFT ] (top-bottom) *untitled* (c. 1917) oil on canvas; and *White Petunia* (1952, block cut 1932) color woodblock print.

ABOVE ] *Painting VII* (1927) oil on canvas.

TOP, RIGHT ] Lazzell (1926) painting at her studio, Provincetown, MA.

She was also included in dozens of other exhibitions across the country. Since her death, her work has been the subject of retrospective exhibitions in Provincetown and at the Creative Arts Center in Morgantown, West Virginia. Martin Diamond Fine Arts in New York has devoted several solo exhibitions to Lazzell and in 2002 Lazzell's prints were celebrated in the touring exhibition *From Paris to Provincetown: Blanche Lazzell and the Color Woodcut* that originated at the Boston Museum of Fine Arts. Most recently, her work is touring in two exhibitions: *Blanche Lazzell: The Hofmann Drawings* and *Blanche Lazzell: The Work of an American Modernist*, curated by Robert Bridges, for which there is a book-length catalog published by the West Virginia University Press with support from the West Virginia Humanities Council – a state affiliate of the National Endowment for the Humanities. Her work is in the collections of the Boston Museum of Fine Arts, the Amon Carter Museum, the Whitney Museum of American Art, the Metropolitan Museum, the Cleveland Museum, the Huntington Museum, the Avampato Discovery Museum at the Clay Center and the West Virginia University Art Collection.

Lazzell is remembered as an early practitioner of modernism in America. She created some of the first non-objective prints and paintings in this country. Though her contribution to American art history was never fully appreciated during her life, recently there has been renewed interest in her work. Blanche Lazzell is respected for the quality of her work, for her important role as a translator of the achievements of European modernism for her colleagues in America and for her innovative and personal abstract style.

[Contributed by Kristina Olson, Assistant Professor of Art, Division of Art, West Virginia University.]

# Richard Kidwell Miller

Photo: William Goidell

RICHARD K. MILLER, a native of Fairmont, began painting at the age of six. During his first few years of school he won several prizes for his work and painted murals throughout the building. He took evening classes at a community art center when it opened and later was allowed to leave school early to take classes there in the afternoon. At the age of 10, one of his paintings, *Still Life*, was selected for an exhibition of juvenile art at the Metropolitan Museum of Art.

In 1943, Miller's family moved to Washington, D.C., and he soon became the youngest artist ever granted permission to copy Old Master paintings in the National Gallery of Art. During the next two years, he won scholarships to study art in Washington and Provincetown, Massachusetts. At the age of 17, Miller came home to Fairmont to attend the opening of his first one-man show at Fairmont State College.

Miller received the Gerturde Vanderbilt Whitney scholarship which provided funds for five years of college study. He spent one year at the Pennsylvania Academy for the Fine Arts and the next four years at American University, where he graduated in 1953. He later earned a Fulbright Fellowship to study in Europe and another Whitney scholarship to pursue a master's degree at Columbia.

In 1960, Miller had a solo exhibition at New York's Duveen Graham Gallery. The following year, he was invited to exhibit at the famous Carnegie International, where his huge abstraction, *Strata*, was selected as one of the top 21 paintings out of 300 entries. While most of his work is abstract in nature, in the late 1980s, he returned to representational art when he began to think his abstract work was becoming too predictable.

## HOMETOWN
### West Virginia

FAIRMONT

In the '90s, he returned to abstraction after becoming influenced by African and Native American art forms. At 73, Miller continues to paint on a daily basis.

In addition to his painting, Miller has enjoyed two other professions. He has taught art at the Kansas City Art Institute in Missouri, the Scarsdale Studio School, Westchester Community College and the Jewish Community College of Mid-Westchester, all in New York. He also spent 20 years acting, appearing in the long-running Broadway production of *Oliver* as well as countless other shows all across the country. Miller has said he found acting became inspirational and interwoven with his love of painting.

[Contributed by John A. Cuthbert, Curator and Director, West Virginia and Regional History Collection and Special Collections, West Virginia University Libraries.]

Photo: Edward J. Avery

OPPOSITE, LEFT ] *Self Portrait* (1944)

OPPOSITE, BOTTOM ] *Glass and Grape* (1986)

ABOVE ] Miller as Fagin in the Broadway musical *Oliver* (1965).

## FROM THE SOUL

Photo: Howard Ross

A beautiful country – a loving family – an older brother and sister about to go to college – a poor, but happy mother and father – we all had a marvelous time. Many playmates at age 6 and 7, but for some reason, I wanted to paint pictures.

In the 4th grade, a great teacher named Mrs. Parker read to the class for a half-hour each morning, everything from *Heidi* to American history. She instilled in me a life-long love of literature and a great desire to paint the Swiss Alps. I covered the school with scenes of the Alps and other images.

A community arts center opened in Fairmont in 1939. A progressive art teacher named Ernest Freed and his equally talented wife made the art center a never ending source of learning and pleasure for me. I learned to paint in oil-landscapes, portraits, still-lifes and figure paintings. At age 11, a painting of mine was chosen to show at the Metropolitan Museum in New York City. I won prizes in every exhibition I entered. All this was my West Virginia introduction to my life as an artist. Nothing could have prepared me better for the years of painting accomplishments – of awards and rewards to come.

*Richard Kidwell Miller*

# Michael K. Paxton

MICHAEL K. PAXTON was born in Huntington, West Virginia, in 1953, the son of fifth generation West Virginians Emerald and Pauline.

He grew up in Logan, Raleigh and Wayne Counties in West Virginia and graduated from Vinson High School in 1971. He received a B.A. in Art from Marshall University in 1975 and a MFA in Drawing and Painting from the University of Georgia in 1979. In 1981, while still in Athens, Georgia, Michael had a one person show at the N.A.M.E. Gallery, Chicago, and was a visiting artist at The School of the Art Institute, Chicago. He moved to Chicago in 1983 where he has maintained a studio for 21 years and resides with his partner Jeanne Nemcek. For 10 years he was represented by Byron Roche Gallery, Chicago, where he had four one person shows and numerous group exhibitions. In 2005 he joined gescheidle Gallery in Chicago and was presented in a one person show of wall-size drawings titled *The Perfume of Shadows*.

Paxton's large traveling painting installation titled *From Enoch to Strange Creek* deals with his family's long history in Clay and Braxton Counties of West Virginia and has been featured at the Chicago Cultural Center; Muskegon Museum of Art, Michigan; Miami University of Art, Oxford, Ohio; Laura Mesaros Gallery, West Virginia University, Morgantown, West Virginia and the Stifel Fine Arts Center, Wheeling, West Virginia.

Michael's work has been featured in many one-person and invitational group exhibitions across the country. His awards include grants from the Illinois Arts Council, the Chicago Department of Cultural Affairs, and the Adolph & Esther Gottlieb Foundation.

In 1998, Michael was commissioned by Jensen Metal Products Inc. of Racine, Wisconsin, to produce a 28' x 72' mural for its corporate headquarters. Other commissioned works include a mural for the Vice President's conference room, 7th District Federal Reserve Bank in downtown Chicago.

Michael began as an Adjunct Instructor in Fine Art at Columbia College, Chicago, in 2005 and over

## HOMETOWN
### West Virginia

#### HUNTINGTON

his long career has been featured as a visiting artist at several colleges and universities. A noted public speaker, he has given numerous lectures on his work and has been featured on radio and television, as well as major newspapers and art journals.

OPPOSITE, LEFT ] *Rev. Jesse*

TOP, LEFT ] *Whispering Eastside*

TOP, RIGHT ] *Throwing the Switch Ball*

LEFT ] *Michael in his studio.*

## FROM THE SOUL

It's hard to sift through a life to see if one persevered because of a situation or despite it. Many times the taller the mountain, the stronger the climber has to become.

My education began in a three-room schoolhouse in Logan County where three teachers taught six grades. They would instruct one side of the room for one grade level and then the other. Listening ahead as much as working on the problem at hand has left me with reading and spelling abilities that are suspect, while my abilities to listen, remember, think in the abstract and decipher the root meaning of things have always been keen.

In junior and senior high school my erratic energy overflow was a puzzlement to most. Participating in band, becoming editor of the school newspaper, student body president, drama club and more was a search for a home for my overpowering creative needs. Mr. Long, art instructor, Mr. Heaberlin, English teacher, Ms. Hodge, drama club director and Mr. Riley, bandleader, tried to help me find focus for my desire to do something, make a difference. However, most of the time this yearning was seen as something I would grow out of because no one from there had ever become a real artist.

It wasn't until my first semester at Marshall University when Ms. June Kilgore spent just a few minutes to impress on me that what I craved really could happen. That art was a great thing and, with hard work and a honing of skills, a life's work awaited me. I still hear her words each and every day. The power of one person caring and positive encouragement is the power that changes lives.

Without the positive words and deeds of a few dedicated people, the toughness and work ethic I learned from my parents and just a little good luck, I wonder if you would be reading this now. Art is a life force. Without positive affirmation and the opportunity to experience and make art, I wonder how many children of West Virginia like me have been and will be lost.

*Michael K. Potter*

# Christopher Sperandio

CHRISTOPHER SPERANDIO is an artist working in a number of distributed media forms including comic books, television and movies.

Born in Kingwood, West Virginia, in 1964, he's the youngest of Opal and Lawrence Sperandio's three children. Inspired by the drawings made by his older brother, and motivated by a love for comics, animation and filmmaking, Mr. Sperandio attended West Virginia University to pursue an education in art. Graduating in 1987 with a Bachelor of Fine Arts degree, he moved to Chicago and attended University of Illinois, Chicago, the following year where he received a Master of Fine Arts degree in painting in 1991.

It was at the University of Illinois where he began a still-ongoing business partnership with British artist Simon Grennan. Confounding typical expectations and bridging cultural and economic boundaries, Grennan and Sperandio's drawings, books and films are rooted mainly in anecdotes of everyday experience. Their collaborative work has been shown extensively throughout Europe and the United States in venues such as the John Weber Gallery; New York's Museum of Modern Art; London's Institute for Contemporary Art, American Fine Arts; the Gallery of Modern Art, Glasgow; the Museum of Fine Arts, Boston; and the Aarhus Kunstsmuseum, Denmark.

Based in New York City, Mr. Sperandio's recent endeavors include several TV pilots for MTV, including animated comedies and a new take on reality television.

# HOMETOWN
## West Virginia

### KINGWOOD

# FROM THE SOUL

A contributing artist at Wired Magazine, he drew the cover of the May 2001 issue and is the co-author of over a dozen comic books published in conjunction with comic book publishers Fantagraphics Books and DC Comics. Mr. Sperandio is currently a Visiting Artist at the nation's top private art college, the School of the Art Institute of Chicago, where he makes occasional visits to advise graduate students across all media disciplines.

Mr. Sperandio lectures on his artwork and working practices internationally and he cultivates mentoring relationships with young artists who want to make a career in the arts. Mr. Sperandio hopes to return to West Virginia to establish an artists' colony where artists of local, national and international significance are provided with the opportunity to make new artworks in the context of the state's natural scenic beauty and warm hospitality of its people – while providing an educational resource for local communities as well as young artists from across the region.

Currently, Sperandio is executive producer and creator of a television show called *Artstar*, the first ever unscripted TV show set in the New York art world. The show will search for the best undiscovered visual artists.

The West Virginia University Press is publishing a monograph about Sperandio and his collaborator called *KARTOON KINGS: The Graphic Work of Simon Grennan and Christopher Sperandio*. The book is due out in the Fall of 2005.

OPPOSITE, TOP ] *The Invisible City* comic book produced for the Public Art Fund, New York (1999).

RIGHT ] Sperandio's *Self-portrait*.

My early creativity was fed by a steady diet of comic books and television.

I bought my first Super 8 camera in 1975 for $35 at Watkin's camera store on Main Street in Kingwood, and was immediately hooked on image making.

The best resource available to me was the Kingwood Public Library, where I began to read about filmmaking and animation. The librarian, Joel Beane, encouraged me, and my buddies Mike Kurilko and Kevin McGuire, to use the A/V equipment the library had, and he even let us shoot our movies in the basement.

The movies we made weren't exactly good, by any standard, but we had fun making them.

The 4-H extension agent Conrad Arnold also helped to support my interests. Where most of the kids in Preston County were doing farming-related projects, Conrad took special effort to help me do photography and movie-making projects.

I was an average student in school, but the enthusiasms that I developed for visual culture – and the crucial early support that I got from the public library and from 4-H – helped me to get into West Virginia University on a talent scholarship and led, eventually, to a career as an artist.

# Whitlatch
Don

For most of his life, DON WHITLATCH ignored his talent for painting. After graduating from Parkersburg High School in 1950, he delivered ice, worked as a janitor and labored in a steel factory. Don didn't know what he was going to do, but his Uncle Sam did.

Following the Korean War, Don, his wife, Norma, and their baby settled in Athens, Ohio, where he studied art at Ohio University. "They wanted square apples and purple bananas," said Don. "I never understood this kind of art." He later enrolled in West Virginia University's pre-dental program. After a year, Norma, a registered nurse, convinced him that he was not "dental material."

Moving home to Parkersburg, he found work as an outdoor billboard painter. Four years later he joined a newly formed advertising agency as creative director, layout man and production supervisor. "Advertising was very frustrating and demanding. It often called for working ten hour days and entertaining clients half the night, making for a very short burning candle."

Quitting the ad game, he started his own design studio and was on his way to a successful career until a heart attack stopped him cold – his rambling days were over. What was he to do now? "Paint wildlife," said Norma. "That's what you know and that's what you love to do."

Now with four children, Norma returned to nursing while Don taught himself the theories of composition, line, color and balance. He chose birds as his main subject. Working with pencil and pad, he would sketch from life the everyday scenes that pass so many of us by. From his log cabin studio he created watercolor images of great detailed realism that soon became known in the art world as "pin-feather" perfect. His is an art that is believable – art that does not have to be explained.

He was soon encouraged to reproduce his work in the form of museum-quality, limited edition, signed and numbered prints. With a network of dealers, galleries and personal shows across America and collectors from five continents, Don was on his way to becoming internationally known and respected. Former Governor Arch

## PARKERSBURG

Moore, Jr., proclaimed Don the first wildlife Artist-In-Residence for the State of West Virginia; a position Don held for seventeen years. He presented an American Bald Eagle painting to the White House in 1974. The piece is now on permanent display at the Nixon Library.

In the mid-nineties, Don was diagnosed with macular degeneration, losing sight in his left eye. Refusing to retire, he decided that it was time to change course. After 25 years, he switched his medium from watercolors to oils and his attention from wildlife to famous golf holes. First came the 3rd at The Cascades Course at the Homestead Resort in Hot Springs, Virginia. Next, the Pete Dye Club at Bridgeport, West Virginia, and then the 16th at Augusta National, home of The Masters. There he met legendary golfers Sam Snead, Gene Sarazen and Byron Nelson who each signed every one of his *Starters* print edition. "The greatest thrill of my life, I think," said Don.

Don and Norma Whitlatch still call Parkersburg home. In 2001, Don's name was permanently placed on a prominent gallery in the new Parkersburg Art Center.

OPPOSITE, LEFT | *Golden Eagle*

OPPOSITE, INSET | Don with Slammin' Sammy Snead.

ABOVE | *The Starters*

# FROM THE SOUL

Stemming from financial reasons, no one in my family ever attended college before me. Getting a job, not an education, was expected of us. It was the time of the Great Depression, and earning a living was hard enough. I regret starting off on the wrong foot in college and not completing any formal degree.

Like all children do, I enjoyed every minute of smearing paint and crayons in elementary school. What dad didn't tear up, my teachers hung up. I guess I never took art seriously as an occupation. I thought it was something everyone did just for the fun of it, not for a living. If it had not been for their encouragement throughout school, I probably would have never become an artist.

To become an accomplished artist you must first compare your work with that of others in your chosen field, be it visual, musical, dancing, acting, writing or whatever. If you are honest with yourself, and you must be, you will soon know if your talents are well worth pursuing.

As a member of the board of directors, I have now turned my "talents" to the cause of educating and promoting regional interest in the new Parkersburg Arts Center. It's a new face in an old building and takes a "back seat" to no other art center in the country. It's for the kids – a place where they can enjoy and learn "how-to." It's for the adults – a place where they can learn to appreciate and cherish the many talents of local and visiting artists from all over the country.

I often hear and enjoy repeated remarks from visitors, such as "I can't believe it, this is beautiful;" "I never knew we had a place like this;" and "Is this really a Rembrandt...right here in Parkersburg?"

There is a lot more to see and learn across West Virginia. Just take the time to look.

Appalachian Education Initiative
# Championing Change in Arts Education

APPALACHIAN EDUCATION INITIATIVE (AEI), founded in December 2001, is a not-for-profit organization committed to furthering arts education in West Virginia public schools and communities. AEI's board of directors is comprised of educators, arts specialists and business and corporate executives, all of whom are dedicated to keeping the arts a fundamental component in West Virginia schools.

The core mission of AEI is to strengthen the role of arts education in the public schools by promoting the essential role of arts education to a child's personal development, academic performance and workforce preparation. AEI spearheads, underwrites and supports education advocacy and research services designed to facilitate and expand arts education programming to benefit children throughout West Virginia.

Volumes of scientific studies exist documenting the positive effects of arts learning on a child's cognitive abilities, social skills and motivation to learn. Systematic application of the arts to a child's education, beginning at the elementary school level, enhances social development and fosters the multiple intelligences in children. By providing a complete education to our children, which includes the arts, we maximize their potential to become vital contributors to the community and the workforce as adults.

All of the proceeds from the purchase of *Art and Soul: West Virginians in the Arts* will be designated for the benefit of AEI programs and services in West Virginia's public schools and communities.

**Appalachian Education Initiative**
111 High Street
Morgantown, West Virginia 26505

www.appalachianeducationinitiative.org